THE
CLYDESDALE
IN THE ATTIC

"*There's a Clydesdale in the Attic* is Donna Cronk's most delightful and charming book yet. The treasures she finds while cleaning out her attic serve as a passageway for memories to surface that the reader can relate to on many levels. Tap-dancing shoes come out of the box and come alive with her charming memories of days as a youth on the family farm near Liberty, Indiana. The stories are uplifting and inspiring, putting a smile on the faces of readers. A must read."

—*Sandy Moore, author and journalist*

"Sorting through the flotsam and jetsam of everyday objects once used by everyday people in their everyday lives, Donna asks, do we keep them, donate them, or trash them? Going through the process reveals a lot about ourselves. This collection of her experiences with her own 'attic treasures' takes readers on an easygoing—and frequently humorous—journey leading to deep universal truths. Her insights make readers thirst for more."

—*Steve Dicken, author, writer, and career English teacher*

"Reading *There's a Clydesdale in the Attic* is like chatting with a good friend, one who entertains you with her discoveries made while sorting through what has collected in her attic, in addition to sharing universal insights gleaned along the way. Since I grew up on a farm, Donna's musings brought back especially sweet memories for me."

—*Cathy Shouse, journalist and author*

"When incredible storyteller, Donna Cronk, cleans out decades of possessions stored in her attic, the result is pure inspiration. As only this award-winning journalist could do, Cronk has compiled a book filled with personal accounts about the origin and significance of each belonging, while offering a valuable practical or spiritual lesson from it. Some of the narratives made me laugh, while others touched me so deeply, I cried. In the end, whether an item ends up being labeled trash or treasure, each heartwarming story reminds the reader to embrace their own poignant memories acquired during the changing seasons of life. This insightful book would be a perfect fit for discussion for a women's book club or church group!"

—*Christina Ryan Claypool, author and inspirational speaker*

"Donna Cronk has the gift of finding the compelling twist of everyday things in life, the telling detail, and then presenting that in a delectable format to the reader."

—*Lisa Perry, journalist, author, and educator*

"Donna has stirred up many memories for me in her new book. You see, I also grew up in Brownsville. I experienced many of the things Donna speaks about. Brownsville was then, and still is, a wonderful place to be. Donna captures the wonderful country life we experienced. Those of us who have moved away due to jobs or other reasons are able to relive our childhoods in her book. Wonderful read!"

—*Melody Gault, career librarian*

THERE'S A
CLYDESDALE
IN THE ATTIC

THERE'S A
CLYDESDALE
IN THE ATTIC

Reflections on Keeping and Letting Go

DONNA CRONK

A MEMOIR OF SORTS

For Brian, my husband and muse, who encourages me to find what makes me happy, not realizing that it's he who does.

Table of Contents

INTRODUCTION

Up the ladder

WELCOME TO MY JOURNEY, complete with numerous ups and downs. A little attic humor there. This book began not with thoughts of a manuscript, but with a different project: of finally cleaning out our attic, along with closets, drawers, and other spaces where stuff collects and seems to reproduce in the night.

Husband Brian and I had been unable to part with many things we had accumulated over the decades, including items saved from our parents, our kids, and keepsakes tucked away from our own lifetimes of experiences. Can you relate?

We had tried the one-fell-swoop method of organizing. Emphasis on *tried*. One summer day we stormed the place, marching single-file, up the rickety pull-down service ladder inside our garage, a fierce two-person team of special operatives.

Once up the stairs though, reality hit, along with the stifling temperature of a July attic. In that moment, we surveyed dozens of containers, each brimming with keepsakes from multiple generations, overflowing with seasonal decorations, paperwork, kids' trophies, toys—the kinds of things I'm guessing that you keep in your storage spaces.

"It's too much," one of us said flatly.

"We can't do this today," the other concurred, wanting to add, "or ever."

A year or few passed, and while discussing the overhead situation, I told Brian about a new idea: enter the attic weekly, select one container, go through it thoroughly, touch each item once, decide to keep it or not. Rinse and repeat until it's done.

My idea, my project. However, I planned to ask Brian and our adult sons what to do with *their* things when I came upon them, and to make no editorial comment about their decisions. In return, they refrained from judgment about what belongings I kept.

To our surprise, it worked! I came to look forward to this time spent sorting. Sometimes, I'd even go through two totes a week. Or, if especially in the zone, three.

What I discovered among the miscellaneous possessions were not hidden treasures of great monetary value. Instead, I found memory prompts for stories about people behind the objects and related blessings that have staying power, whether a specific item remains with us or not.

As I made these discoveries, the project led to this one: a book. It's about what I unpacked along with the stuff. The nice thing about stories is they don't take up much space—at least they don't until the book boxes arrive. But that's a whole other issue, and I can't wait for that journey, and hearing readers share *their* stories.

On that note, there's a special section in the back for book clubs' discussions—or for personal contemplation.

WANT TO KNOW HOW Brian accidentally inspired the book title?

I'm an early riser, and in summer, the sun is my sidekick. During the season of cleaning out, I'd head up the stairs after dawn one morning a week, generally on Fridays or Saturdays, before the heat set in, and get to work. Sometimes that meant reorganizing the ever-increasing number of newly empty containers, as well as restacking the reorganized ones directly over the garage and our bedroom.

Brian spent his career leaving for work before dawn. In retirement, he enjoys sleeping in. Sunrise finds him blissfully snoozing. One morning I returned downstairs from my weekly exploit and nonchalantly entered our bedroom.

"What are you *doing* up there?" he mildly grumbled while still in bed, head affixed to the pillow.

"Cleaning the attic. Why, did you hear me?" Apparently I had been a bit overzealous in my work.

"It sounds like a Clydesdale up there stomping around," he said, never opening his eyes.

Amused by my husband's version of sweet talk, I thought: *Well, it probably does, at that.*

While there were many things stashed inside our attic, along with inside other storage spaces, rest assured that no actual Clydesdales were harmed in the making of this book.

This isn't a story of collectors who became minimalists. Not hardly! Going through everything brought clarity about what to keep and what to let go, at least for us at this stage of our lives. It's never a final work. We kept plenty. We're okay with that.

Before I show you around, how about some background? I grew up on a family farm in tiny Union County, Indiana. Where's that? Ever hear of Liberty or Brownsville? Probably not, unless you're from that area of east-central Indiana. My farmer father, Huburt, also drove a school bus for decades. He married a young woman named Martha from nearby Richmond who became a rural homemaker and my mother. Mom figured she'd eventually get Dad back to *her* hometown, but, country life grew on her. When they semi-retired, and had the chance to move to town, she couldn't do it.

Mom loved the Lord, my dad, our family, her church, and summer zinnias. Turns out she also loved our farm.

Brian is my spouse of more than forty years. He spent his career as a secondary public school administrator and teacher. Other names you'll see often on these pages, along with Brian and our folks, are those of our sons, Sam and Ben. Sam arrived first with younger brother Ben coming along a few years later. They're grown and on their own, but their presence is always with us, whether inside our hearts or visiting our home. And, it remains inside our attic.

You'll hear stories about Brian's parents, Ray and Mary, who, as mine, have passed on. They were salt-of-the-earth Hoosiers. They loved each other and their family dearly, along with enjoying a long, loving marriage.

Sweet-spirited Mary relished homemaking, becoming known for her cooking and baking, including melt-in-your-mouth fruit pies. I especially loved her spaghetti-laden chili.

A country boy from rural Parke County, Ray served in the U.S. Army during World War II as a tank driver in every major battle on the European front. After the war, back home again, he supported his family for decades working at the Standard Oil Refinery in Whiting before returning with Mary to Parke County where they enjoyed retirement.

As for yours truly, I started writing as a kid, taking second place for my first essay which related to community history. Don't hate me for what memory serves was a seven-dollar prize. I know of only two other entrants. I can name them both.

While a check for seven bucks was nice at the time, the enduring reward is that essay, laminated in all its runner-up glory, thanks to a mother who saved most everything.

Even better is the local-and-family history represented on those pages, of growing up in the rural-Indiana place that is now a long-ago life chapter. It was my world. Where does the time go? I ask that almost daily these days.

AT SIXTEEN, I KNEW that one day I wanted to become a newspaper reporter. I never sought to be anything else professionally, and feel blessed to have spent thirty-seven years telling people's stories on the pages of community newspapers.

The stories in this book, however, are personal. Yes, it is possible to both clean out an attic, and find joy in that journey. The heavy lifting is done. The heaviest thing you'll hoist regarding this little book is this little book—or maybe your favorite beverage while reading it. Then again, you might get some ideas about what *you* can do to make sense of your own stored-and-storied stuff, and think about the people, experiences, and lessons that have informed your life and times.

Okay then, consider yourself properly prepped. You've stayed this long, so please, hang out with me the rest of the way.

If you're still game—let's head up the ladder, shall we?

1

Two of a kind

BRIAN AND I ARE keepers. We come from a long line of them. Our Midwestern parents and grandparents were deeply affected by the Great Depression. They weren't wealthy people, but rather hardscrabble Hoosiers who conducted streetcars and drove school buses, grew crops, raised livestock, and supported their families through physical labor. Their possessions took hard work and time to obtain.

For folks of their era and lifestyles, once you worked to earn something, you appreciated what you had, cared for it, and used it well. Possessions weren't quickly upgraded for what's newer or better. If you no longer needed something, the item wasn't discarded, nor sold at a yard sale. Instead, it went into the back of a cabinet, high on a shelf, or into the barn because one day you might need it again. Or your family members might. The term "being good stewards" comes to mind.

We inherited many of our parents' well-used belongings, but

also our ancestors' attitudes about these objects. That's why when Brian cleared out our garage during our season of paring down, he set out to organize each wrench, bucket, and unidentified, metal thingy so well that he can go straight to it when the need arises. I think there's even an Unidentified Metal Thingies section. You know if you throw away one of those thingies, you will soon need it.

He planned to finally part with a partially filled, scruffy-looking tin of a petroleum product that his dad, Ray, had kept. The container survived multiple moves and six decades riding high on one garage shelf after another, landing on ours.

With it, as with most all our belongings, comes a memory. Brian recalls as a kid, his dad brought home a supply of this product, advertised as the answer to many kinds of household cleaning-or-lighting needs.

But wait. We still have the tin! I thought Brian got rid of it with other random cans of chemically based liquids by hauling them to our local recycling site. When asked about it, he said no—he took the others—but decided to hang onto this one.

I'm not sure if he kept it in his father's memory, or because of that deeply ingrained belief that even after all these years and moves, and although I don't believe it has ever been used in our household, it's got potential; it's wasteful to dispose of something with potential.

EARLY ON IN THIS decluttering process, I went through our sons' baby toys while sitting on the attic floor at the top of the stairs. The plastic objects took me back to those early days of motherhood.

Each item that I pulled out had been forgotten until I held it again, deeming it suddenly familiar as I evaluated it for keeping or donating. Holding a small, wheeled ride, I recalled Sam's first word after da-da and ma-ma: truck.

Baby rattles, plastic vehicles, and a noisy activity board that attaches to a crib went back into the bin, keepsakes all.

There might be children one day who will enjoy playing with their parents' first toys. If not, the items can easily be donated for another baby to use. There is a timelessness to the simplicity of a classic toy.

Still, this whole cleaning-out business is pointless if there isn't anything to part with from storage. Here I am, getting started with the project, and already struggling with the reality of letting go.

Finally, I found something: a squeaky, bathtub toy. The boys had played with the plastic fish when they were toddlers enjoying their baths. I released the tubby toy, letting it fall from my perch onto the concrete floor below.

About then, Brian stepped from the house into the garage where he spotted the toy lying there.

"What's this?" he asked, picking it up, then answering his own question. "Looks like one of the boy's tubby toys." Funny how old baby-talk expressions come back to us. With a decisive air, I told Brian that I'm donating it. *Yessir, that's exactly what I'll do*, I thought.

I kept sorting, but as I did, I noticed that Brian still held the toy as he turned back toward the house. I overheard him mumble, "I can't throw *that* away."

Remembering our rule not to quibble about what gets saved, I said nothing.

Brian relocated it to a top shelf inside his bedroom closet. The toy seems to keep watch from its unlikely safe space; saved by one sentimental father.

CLEANING OUT IS HARD when you throw it out—and then save it anyway.

The cleaning product from my father-in-law? I could let *that* go. Yet, it wasn't my call. However, what good is it after all these years, its exterior dusty and scratched? Did the product even work if the occasion ever arose to try it?

I found out—and ate my words.

A couple months after the petroleum-tin discussion, I painted the trim around our exterior garage doors. Suddenly, I made a mess, spilling and splattering paint. I quickly looked around our garage. How to clean it up, and quickly? Might this require a trip to the hardware store? Ugh!

Then I remembered the ancient cleaning product, still biding its time on our shelf. I opened the tin, used the solution, and fancy that: it worked perfectly. Its outer appearance and age had nothing to do with its interior worth and strength.

From somewhere in heaven, Ray Cronk got the last laugh.

2

Family artifacts aren't about price tags

WHILE BRIAN'S DAD LOVED to fish, he didn't care to eat his catch. At some point, maybe forty, fifty, or even more years ago, Ray took special pride in a trio of largemouth bass he had caught, and mounted their heads on a piece of scrap board as a makeshift trophy.

We're not sure the significance of these fish, but Brian thinks they represent an especially good single day wetting a line. They probably also have to do with memories enjoying his favorite pastime. How he loved fishing in rural, southern Indiana on warm summer nights, the work week behind him. Accompanying Ray on these trips were his favorite fishing buddies: his brother Tut, or an assortment of brothers-in-law who were equally dear.

The handmade trophy hung inside my father-in-law's garage for decades. During the auction of his household belongings, the fishes were mixed in with boxes of sellable goods, then removed and left behind following the sale as so much garbage. After the auction ended and we cleaned up the remains, I tossed the board onto a heap of rubble, destined for next week's trash truck.

That evening, when Brian heard about my trashing the trophy, he couldn't rest until he returned to the property to search for it. When he finally dug it out of the heap, the fishes' heads were worse for the wear, but remarkably intact considering what they had just been through. They are inside our attic today.

During the recent cleaning spree, I had the good sense not to ask if Brian planned to keep this heirloom. That had been established.

But do I understand keeping such a relic? I sure do. The trophy meant more to my father-in-law than any professionally engraved plaque could have. He saw not a wood scrap, but a piece of his past, a reminder of his best days. After my mistake of tossing it, and Brian's reaction, I realized that the son saw his father in those fish remnants.

The homemade trophy is a tangible reminder of my husband's love for his pop. I'm glad that Brian regards the attic as near enough for this heirloom though, and that he hasn't suggested an upgrade in, say, the living room.

Some of us feel the need to keep those select pieces from the past in physical form. Others of us do not.

WE HUMANS KEEP ARTIFACTS from our lives that may strike others as odd. Yet when you think about it, it's not so different from contents inside museums and landmarks the world over, devoted to noteworthy people and their lifestyles. In those settings we examine and hear stories about their belongings as we long to understand and somehow feel closer to them. We ooh and aah. We buy the T-shirt in the gift shop.

But sometimes, we're prone to make light of our own family's humble keepsakes, even though we often learn so much from them.

Consider our sleigh bells. Brian and I have never once hopped aboard a horse-drawn sleigh, yet we keep those bells, which had been tucked away for decades on their well-worn leather strap, inside my folks' utility closet.

Farm horses and ponies of common stock were a big part of Dad's and his father's lives in the early half of the previous century. Grandpa farmed with draft horses. As kids growing up, my father, brothers, and I had ponies of our own. They weren't for showing in competitions, but for riding and enjoying casually.

While I've long since physically left the farm, and a childhood spent with equines, I once asked Mom if I could keep those sleigh bells. When she agreed, I promptly found a leatherworker specializing in tack to restring them onto a new, black belt. For two decades they have stretched out the length of our entryway wall.

Those bells are reminders of farm eras when horses and ponies played roles in everyday life and rural culture. There was a time when country kids hopped on their ponies and took off down a gravel road as I did, accompanied by our dog, Penny, and our three-legged cat, Tiger, trailing behind. Penny could go the distance, whatever that turned out to be, but Tiger couldn't keep up and soon turned back.

Another family-farm relic is a large dinner bell. For the longest time it sat inside Dad's barn, and then, inside a corner of our garage. *It should go or be mounted on a post in our backyard*, I thought for years before it happened. It's on a post now, a tribute to a farming heritage, and during the writing of this book, I planted marigolds around it where they bloomed with gusto all summer. You see numerous old dinner bells displayed throughout the Indiana countryside.

Of course, there's no practical need, as with the sleigh bells, for such an object to remain on our property. The bell is a nod to the past, of a time when Grandma called Grandpa to the table when he worked inside the barn or in the fields. When the bell rang, he knew to go home for dinner (the midday meal) or supper (the evening meal). Or maybe Grandma sounded the bell if she needed him to come quickly, such as in an emergency.

Both the string of sleigh bells and the dinner bell nurture scenarios not from my memory bank, but rather from my imagination. Envisioned is a time when on the childhood homeplace, horses pranced, bells jingling as they pulled sleighs, and Grandma paged Grandpa by ringing the bell, as one might use a cellphone today.

I also inherited a slate chalkboard, bought at auction from the 1912 Brownsville schoolhouse where Dad, my two brothers, and I attended school. I barely made the cut, attending summer kindergarten there shortly before the school closed due to consolidation.

When the school corporation sold the township building's contents more than half a century ago, my quirky father purchased the blackboards. All of them. He took a smaller piece of one and moved it into my bedroom where I spent hours playing school and doodling on that board. Many years later, I had it framed, and hung it on the kitchen wall for our children to play with.

In recent years, it has remained unused, propped against a garage wall. Rather than sell it at a future garage sale, I gave it to Jim, someone from my hometown who is the unofficial keeper of local history. I'm tickled to see the slate return to its hometown.

THERE ARE MANY REASONS why we save oddities, some of them ridiculous. I have never been able to part with my high school cap and gown. Royal blue and still in perfect condition, together they make a slim package in their original plastic wrap.

The package went into Mom's cedar chest after I got the diploma. Why did I keep it? I probably thought a relative might save a few bucks using it when she graduated from the same high school, but then I forgot about it. I've come close to tossing it during one cleaning spree or another. But the tidy twosome always makes the cut and stays.

The last time I considered letting go of these relics from the momentous event of graduating from high school, I decided to keep them. Here's my reasoning. (Please hold your laughter until I've left the chapter.) I thought the invite might eventually arrive to attend a Halloween masquerade party. I'd go as a graduate! Outfit is ready and it's free. (Ahem, I'm still in the chapter.)

On the one occasion that I have ever been invited to such a gathering, a kids' party involving our sons, I forgot all about the stored graduation attire. Supervising adults were encouraged to dress up. I had no idea what to wear, so drove to a costume-rental shop where I could surely find a variety of options, right? Wrong!

Exactly one outfit met the criteria of fitting while providing adequate coverage for the mother of two young sons at their party: I could go as a nun.

Frustrated by the single option, I decided to forgo renting a costume and show up as a middle-aged mom. I had the outfits for that; a closet full of them.

It's time to donate that cap and gown. Maybe they will be snapped up by someone looking for a Halloween costume. Or not. One reason we humans have clutter is when we choose to save things for events that *might* happen one day. Yet often those future happenings never come to fruition. And sometimes we realize that we no longer care if they don't—and that in my case—I have no desire to attend a masquerade party.

It's time for the graduation attire to attend someone else's party. Leaving the chapter now. You are free to laugh.

3

The golden letter

EVERYONE CALLED HER GOLDIE. She arrived on the scene seemingly straight from central casting in the role of the fun-loving, adorable grandmother in a situation comedy. Only Goldie wasn't performing the role for TV. This was real life.

As a farm kid in rural Indiana, I didn't often get the chance to meet women such as Goldie. Most adult females I knew of a certain age were quiet farm wives similar to my mother. They had either grown up in the community where we lived or moved there from a nearby town.

My best friend Cheryl's maternal grandmother, Goldie brought a new vibe to the cornfields of our locale. She had spent her earlier years in Cincinnati, then moved to California.

I mean—*California!* If you lived in the Golden State, to me you were closer to being a celebrity than to being any grandmother I knew. Did she know Marcia Brady?

From third grade on, Cheryl and I took turns spending Friday overnights at each other's homes. That continued through much of high school. I loved Fridays at Cheryl's.

While I lived deep in the country with no surrounding houses, Cheryl lived on the edge of Philomath, a small community with several homes nearby on one side of her place, and her family's farm stretching out on the other.

A streetlight beamed outside her house. Granted, it was actually a security light, the electric bill likely paid by her dad—not exactly Times Square—but something appealed about the glow of that evening light. You could see to ride bicycles longer if you wanted, or watch for bats that were attracted to it. Her community also had blacktopped roads, as compared to our farm which bordered dusty, gravel ones.

The fun started when I rode the school bus home with Cheryl. Following supper, we tooled around on her tandem bike, then came in to spend the rest of the evening playing with Barbies. Having so much fun, we stayed at it until we could no longer hold our eyelids open a moment longer. Then it was off to bed, dreaming of our Saturday escapades.

The next day, we might play in the woods, a spot Cheryl called "the sugar camp," so named for the remains of a shack, evidently where someone in her family once processed maple syrup. We might create a variety show on her sidewalk, pretend to launch a community newspaper, or play school in an actual red-brick, one-room schoolhouse on her farm, long since rendered obsolete by the township. Who might you know who had one of *those*?

WHEN WE WERE ABOUT eleven, news came that Goldie planned to visit from her home in California. I hadn't met her yet, but the anticipation was palpable. I quickly learned that this woman enjoyed fun, good times, and adventure. When you were around Goldie, anything could happen—such as receiving a surprise gift.

Remember the five-year diaries, a dollar apiece, each with a lock and tiny key? Goldie bought them for her granddaughters— with an extra for me. From then on, it seemed my duty to record whatever happened on those small pages with even smaller lines. With only a tiny space to pen anything, writing there still became a regular discipline, sometimes recording such insightful notations as, "Nothing happened today." Yet the routine served as a foretaste of my newspaper career when, if something important occurred on my beat, the event wasn't complete until I wrote about it.

During attic cleaning I came across that battered diary, its cover hanging loose, the small key long gone. It documented anxieties of the 'tween years on through age fourteen. Moments of angst, silly stuff, whining, and names of boys, boys, and more boys were recorded on those pages.

A real treasure to keep forever, you might say? Maybe, but after review, the pages felt too personal for others to read or evaluate. I let the diary go, along with its sequel that I continued journaling in throughout high school.

SOMEHOW, I GOT THE idea that Goldie babysat for actors' kids while on the West Coast. We didn't use the word "nanny" back then, at least not in our part of the country. Specifics were fuzzy about for whom Goldie worked, leaving everything to my substantial imagination. To my child's eyes, anything is possible if you're from such a magical place as California.

No matter. I figured details had to remain secret when you were dealing with celebrities' children. Mind you, Goldie never once said any of her employers were *actual* celebrities, but it sure was fun to imagine.

While you'd think that Goldie's nickname obviously resulted from her surname, Goldkiller, you also couldn't help but notice her bright blonde hair. Either way, the moniker suited her.

With her arrival came unique gifts for her granddaughters—along with the diaries. The faux-fur coat for Barbie. The orange-cased, face-powder compact. The beautiful clothes newly hung inside Cheryl's closet. They had *everything* in California and my friend and her sisters benefited from their grandmother's generosity. Also known for her cooking, Goldie introduced into my vocabulary dishes not found in our kitchen at home. Hoagies and bourbon balls come to mind.

For a year or two after I met her, Goldie seemed to venture back and forth between California and our dot on the map. Another daughter and family lived in California, and a third lived an hour's drive from Cheryl's house.

I'LL NEVER FORGET THE February day I came home from school and there on the living room desk sat the bright pink envelope postmarked Santa Monica, California. It held a letter, handwritten to me from Goldie! She asked something that exceeded my wildest dreams: Could I accompany Cheryl to California to visit her that coming summer?

I couldn't believe it! Someone asked *me* to get on a jet airplane and fly with my best friend to the home of Annette Funicello, Lucille Ball, and the whole Brady Bunch. Well, *technically* she didn't mention any of them in particular, but still. We might run into them.

What she did promise were trips to Disneyland, San Francisco, and Mexico! It was too much to imagine for this farm kid who had never been anywhere beyond Cincinnati, sixty miles southeast, or to the Indiana State Fair, eighty miles west.

Even though I knew in my heart that my folks wouldn't let me go to California that summer, I couldn't blame them. It was the idea of being *chosen* that meant everything. To her credit, Mom didn't say no right away, giving me time to savor the possibilities involved. After she finally told me what I had guessed, Mom sent Goldie a note thanking her for the invitation, all the same.

By junior high, Goldie came to permanently live with my friend's family, becoming what we lovingly today call a granny nanny, while Cheryl's parents were at work outside the home.

SOME YEARS LATER, GOLDIE once again invited me on an adventure. This one would be for the two of us. She asked me to be her assistant for a couple of weeks at a summer-camp cooking gig she had landed two towns away.

I said yes, and for two weeks that August, learned about hard work as I trailed my competent boss around the kitchen helping prepare three squares a day for around thirty hungry campers, then clean up after each meal. Soon after that, we started the prep work to do it all over again.

Little time remained for this assistant cook to swim in the lake, fall in love with a camp counselor, or discover whatever else a girl my age thought working at a campground provided.

Goldie and I bunked in twin beds in the same room, steps from the kitchen. By nightfall, my feet were tired, and my body ready to crash from the hectic day. At the end of two weeks, I became fifty bucks richer and recipient of a bonus gift: a back-to-school skirt and coordinating sweater, selected by Goldie.

Fifty dollars was the largest amount of money I had ever received at once.

After graduating from high school, I no longer saw much of Goldie. Life changed with first a part-time job and boyfriend named Brian, and before long, a full-time job and the same boyfriend whom I would marry the following year.

GOLDIE HAS BEEN GONE for years, as have so many key figures from my youth. I wish I could thank her now for the invitation to California, for the diary, and for the summer job preparing all those meals.

We worked hard and I learned how much two people can accomplish in feeding a dining hall full of camper kids and their adult counselors, and how organized my summer boss had to be in pulling off the whole thing so beautifully. I wish I had written down exactly *what* we prepared. I can't recall now, only picturing a blur of chopping, stirring, mixing, and assembling food; yet I seem to recall the camping staff raving about Goldie's meals. No one went hungry, certainly not the assistant cook.

Along with the diary from Goldie, while going through the attic, I came across the invitation to California. Just as this woman had done all those years ago, the bright pink envelope stood out. As I read her note again, I felt as awestruck as when it originally found its way to our farmhouse.

Whether a possible trip to the Pacific Coast, or a summer job, Goldie made me feel welcome and capable. There's a lot to be said for someone who can make you feel both.

A trip to the Golden State has been on my mind two other times—once, as a kid when I'd unrealistically hoped for an invite from my brother, David, on his family's vacation (the car was full), and again—when a travel group we enjoy had begun planning a summer 2020 trip. The vacation had to be canceled due to the pandemic. Ironically, it was the same summer that I found Goldie's letter.

I still have never made it to California.

But if I ever get there, and I hope I do—the first person I think of won't be Marcia Brady or Annette Funicello. It will be, of course, a grandma named Goldie.

4

On tap

IF YOU WERE AMONG the talented girls growing up in my hometown, you took dance lessons at the local studio.

I had numerous friends and family members who enjoyed those lessons, and each year, they participated in a dance review. Mom and I always attended this rite-of-spring program. In that era of the televised variety show, the local program seemed as though it were our own version. Ours featured no Hollywood stars, but rather regular people we knew.

Their colorful sequins sparkled as the dancers tapped, square-danced, and otherwise made their way across the stage in a wide range of peppy numbers; magical to view, and quite the confidence builder if you were a performer.

I wanted to be a performer; especially, a tap dancer.

With our farm located several miles from town, my parents didn't deem dancing important enough to justify the cost in lessons, time, and gas money.

To get it, you will need to understand the time and place of rural Indiana in the late 1960s through the early 1970s. Much needed done on a small farm. There were animals to feed. Fields and fences to see to. Gasoline cost money. Leisure activities off the farm were occasional, even *rare* distractions, not a part of everyday, nor even typical weekend life.

Today, parents encourage their children to get involved in lessons, clubs, and programs of all kinds. Parents want the experiences to build talents and interests, for their offspring to try new things, enjoy their options, create credentials to place on possible college scholarship applications, and maybe see the results in career paths later.

I appreciate that perspective, or at least a balanced version as pertains to allocation of time and resources. It wasn't that way in the home where I grew up—and I understand that my parents' viewpoints simply differed from those in some other families. Of course, I always chalked it up to them being old-fashioned and I honored their views.

THE FOLKS DID, HOWEVER, permit enrollment in 4-H, an organization we knew well in our rural community for programming centered on raising livestock, crops, and learning life skills of many kinds. The acronym stands for Head, Heart, Hands, and Health. During a decade of involvement, I undertook as many as ten projects a year.

These ranged from photography to baking, to sewing dresses and other outfits, to crocheting a colorful lightweight throw, and refinishing furniture. I learned how to grow and arrange flowers; create a terrarium; write skits for the annual Share the Fun talent show; keep good records; and develop leadership skills.

My parents thought I'd learn more practical knowledge in 4-H than in dance, and it meant fewer miles on the car, as our local club met in nearby homes. There were opportunities for camp, demonstrations, trips, Junior Leaders, and yes, we had great fun in the process.

But there were no sequins; no tap shoes; no glitzy dance reviews. A dancer friend from church highlighted her experiences one Sunday, explaining why I should make another pitch to my parents for lessons. I knew it wouldn't matter, that Dad would quickly shut down any nagging.

Besides that, by the time you're in upper elementary school, it's probably too late to catch up with the girls who had danced for years and were destined for coveted positions on the high school cheerleading squad or drill team.

If I couldn't be a dancer trained in all the right moves and perform on a stage, or a cheerleader pepping up a crowd, I could still take matters into my own hands—or onto my own feet, in this case. I devised a plan.

I saved the small earnings from gassing up and sweeping out Dad's school bus (fifteen cents a pop), mowing the lawn (a buck a week, in season), and other odd jobs on the farm, such as removing field rocks so they wouldn't damage equipment, and painting the picket fence.

Finally, I had saved enough for my important purchase. The time had come to visit the mall shoe store and ask to try on a pair of black, patent-leather tap shoes, size six.

No store requirements existed to sign an affidavit stating that I knew what to do with said tap shoes or to provide a learner's permit to use them. Once I produced the cash, they would let even a country bumpkin like me take them home.

Once I had the shoes, back on the farm, I did my best imitation of tap dancing on the kitchen's linoleum floor, on the concrete back porch, and on the front sidewalk. My "lessons" came largely from studying weekly routines on *The Lawrence Welk Show*.

In summer, my nieces and I produced our own variety programs and sold out the front-porch seating for a dime a seat to neighbor kids who came to watch. We sang everything from Sunday school songs to pop music and show tunes, tap dancing our hearts out through each number.

THE OLD TAP SHOES were inside our attic, buried deep at the bottom of a clothing bin that had been saved for decades. Once out of their original box, the shoes appeared in decent shape except for the liners that were too misshapen to stay put. Off came my sneakers and I slipped on the taps—well, squeezed them on, anyway. Sure, they were too small, but only a couple sizes. What's a few cramped toes—ten, maybe—for the sake of artistic expression?

I took them off and carried them down the attic ladder. Half a century after purchasing these long-sought-after shoes, here I stood, a pajama-clad senior citizen, putting on those shoes. I sported the childhood prizes as naturally as though I had worn them two days ago.

Kind of a pathetic scene, I suppose, but not so to me. Just maybe, a joyful one. Either way, you know what happened next.

I took off around that garage tapping my confined toes like there was no tomorrow. After a little while, I took off the shoes. Okay, they hurt my feet. Instead of trashing them, or returning them to the attic, they got an upgrade similar to the tubby toy from a previous chapter. The tap shoes received VIP seating on my closet shelf. But first came a makeover as I buffed them with furniture polish and threaded sparkly, red ribbon through the eyelets.

THE LESSON OF THE tap shoes is about how to react in life when we don't get everything we want when we want it (or ever), and to accept that not everything goes our way. Sometimes life's tap-dance lessons never come.

It's also about creatively finding our own dreams. The shoes are a reminder of life's Plan Bs; of working hard toward our goals. And about how even if you don't find exactly what you want, something else will come along that works just fine—or even better.

True, I never became a dancer. But I got the shoes. And the childhood fun. And, I got to be in 4-H, which turned out as likely a better fit for this country girl, anyway. I didn't know it then, but through 4-H, and our little neighborhood shows, I absorbed skills in creative thinking, organization, and problem solving that I've applied to life.

Today I have a pair of shoes that remind me of all that.

When the sun hits them just right—that patent leather? It still shines.

5

You do you

NOT ONLY DID I save all the "good" school papers from our children's younger years—you know the ones, those with the A's, and the cute stickers, smiley faces, and shiny stars—but I kept a surprising number of my own. In the attic container filled with these old, graded assignments, I happened upon a sweet surprise: a small hand-drawn caricature with my first name neatly printed under it. One glance and I knew exactly where it came from, half a century removed.

Grade five became my favorite year of elementary school as a student in Jeanne Sipahigil's class. Kind and easygoing, she made everything interesting. Students who would spend that year together were welcomed that fall with Mrs. Sipahigil's renderings of each classmate. They were placed on the classroom bulletin board to greet us where they remained until year's end when we took them down for keeps.

As a master teacher, Mrs. Sipahigil had, I speculate now, a

deeper psychological point in mind than decorating the room with cute drawings. We all want to feel a part of something bigger than ourselves. Even, or maybe especially, in elementary school. Not only do we want to belong, we *need* to belong.

The drawings provided a unified front on that bulletin board; we were all in this thing called fifth grade together.

I think most humans, at least in our culture, would agree that there's something disarming, comforting even, about being called by name. That's why our names on those drawings were important.

That year, we put on an American history program, filmed on the in-house television system. The TV set rode high on top of a roll-away cart.

I found the battered script inside our attic, written by our teacher, and printed in purple ink, compliments of the school mimeograph machine. Remember that ink? I always liked the scent of those papers while still "hot off the press," and smelling vaguely of peppermint.

That year, I wrote an essay about the impact of the landing and first walk on the Moon. It is with the same amount of awe I feel today that I wrote about it being the first time a human's feet were planted on firm ground other than on the Earth. Mrs. Sipahigil evidently liked it, because it landed both a good grade and a coveted place on the bulletin board, akin to page one in a newspaper.

GRADE FIVE WAS THE year in those days when students got a special reward—or at least that's how we perceived it. We were each permitted to work in the cafeteria for one week during that school year. Names for the labor pool were drawn the week prior to service.

I waited weekly with great anticipation to learn if I would be selected to spend the noon hour the following week in a hairnet dipping out servings of corn and placing creamed-chicken sandwiches into small squares on pale-green cafeteria trays.

The school year had nearly ended when my call to duty arrived. Elated, I couldn't wait to share my good fortune with Mom. Do you remember that feeling of sprinting off the school bus or running home to give your mother a piece of good news? It's one of life's simple pleasures.

There's something special about getting out of class early and doing something new behind the scenes. One of the school cooks told the custodian that week, "If we can put men on the Moon then we ..." whatever the rest of the story concluded. I recall thinking at the time how that will henceforth be a new phrase that resonates with everyone.

All those are good memories. There is a bad one.

I liked a boy in another class. When he heard through the grade school grapevine that I had a crush on him, he said something unkind, using a word I had never heard before. This was naturally shared with me.

After that, the word he used and its definition were explained, in whispered tones from an older girl on the school bus, a place where we learned from one another about all sorts of things we had never heard of before.

I'm glad I asked her and not my mother! I remain certain that Mom had never heard that word before—and shouldn't.

I could say the word but then your mother would need to wash your ears out with soap.

HOWEVER, THE MOST MEANINGFUL lesson that year has provided useful instruction all my life. I have thought of it in many circumstances, and even this one, the act of writing a book, and wondering how it will fare.

My reading group also met in Mrs. Sipahigil's class. Our assignment one week? To perform a play for one another. Prep involved selecting which part you wanted to tackle, then auditioning. I overlooked the primo characters, going for a minor role.

The part that interested me was that of the winsome dog. I could have some fun with it. Maybe no one else even wanted to portray this unique cast member, but I did. Maybe I'd be a paw in. The night before tryouts, I came up with a concept of how the pooch should approach the storyline. I practiced alone in my room until I became comfortable with my interpretation; so familiar that I couldn't wait until time to show the class my little skit.

When tryouts came, the smartest girl in the class wanted the same part I did. She went first. As she auditioned, the classmates roared with appropriate laughter. When she finished, they all showed their approval with thunderous applause.

I felt raw panic. My turn to perform had at last arrived, but all confidence had been lost after viewing my competitor's interpretation. I had a completely different concept for the role from the one that had just stolen the show.

With all eyes on me, I scrapped my idea as being horrendous and proceeded to render what amounted to a cheap imitation of how my classmate's dog character acted the part.

No laughter, no applause. The room fell silent. I felt humiliated. Of course, the role went to the other girl, as well it should have.

In that moment of disappointment and embarrassment, the lessons began to sink in: don't try to be someone you're not; realize that you're capable of creative concepts that differ from those of your peers; give your ideas a chance and see what happens.

And, if there's a choice, go first. Set the standard that the others will emulate. Or at least, by going first, you know that you've given it your best; done it your way.

Sometimes, the most instructive lessons, the ones that last a lifetime, arrive in surprising ways. Even in grade-five reading class. I failed to get the prize at hand—but the takeaway remains a part of me. Priceless.

A popular phrase today is, "You do you." I learned that the hard way in the fifth grade.

6

---〰〰〰---

Playing dress up

IT DOESN'T GET ANY more Midwestern farm girl than sewing your own prom dress. I didn't even know if I'd have a date when the time came, but I knew this: I most assuredly wanted one, and come spring, I wanted that still-fictional fella, to escort me to the gala.

With each stitch on Mom's sewing machine—nearly a year away from the junior prom—this teenage girl's hope breathed into every stitch of that blue, flowing gown. What girl doesn't want to be a princess going to the ball? A small-school prom is the rural version of both princess and ball.

The formal dress I sewed resembled an earlier, fancy gown in my life, also blue. Mom designed and made it for my Barbie. She stitched it when some of my third-grade classmates decided to have a contest during an upcoming indoor, winter recess.

We'd all vote on the doll who wore the prettiest gown. Unlike national queen pageants we enjoyed viewing on television, this contest came with no title, talent, scholarship, nor swimsuit competition. It was all about the evening wear. We had the weekend to put together our dolls' ensembles. There were no picky rules. I wanted my doll to win.

I asked Mom to create the dress. In that magical way that mothers have, from her fabric scrap box she combined pieces of royal blue fabric with a bit of netting overlay, a little dab of recycled lace, possibly from the hem of a discarded slip, and voila, Barbie would go to the ball. Or at least to Mrs. Orr's midday recess.

I grew up in a home where parents didn't rush to town for expensive supplies for their daughter's every whim. We never considered buying a doll's premade evening gown for this adventure. No, this creation came from my mother's imagination and sewing know-how. It cost nothing, yet everything—in the form of her precious time and expertise.

The Barbie gown surprised me in its perfection. To my delight, it swept the contest.

I CONNECTED THAT GRADE school moment to my first prom dress while delving into the attic container that bulged with now-vintage formal wear. The gown consisted of a light-blue, Dotted Swiss fabric with a similar bodice and sweeping skirt as that long-ago doll formal, trimmed not in leftover lace, but with strips of white feathers rounding the neckline and sleeves.

The idea for the feather trim came from viewing the gown of a beautiful local girl who used a similar accent the year before in the 4-H-fair queen contest.

I envisioned the skirt with a sweep of white feathers around the hem as well as the neckline and sleeves, but didn't push it, as the idea seemed too lavish for my mother's pocketbook.

We were, if nothing else, practical farm folk, and that's why my 4-H-clothing project and anticipated prom dress were one and the same, a textbook example of a favorite lifelong mantra of killing two birds with one stone.

The 4-H-fair payoff consisted of ribbons with the always-unattainable carrot of a silver tray that the grand champion in dress review is awarded. I also longed for a coveted Indiana State Fair sticker, designating the project worthy to represent our county at the state level.

Accessories were a new pair of white high heels (eventually worn at our wedding), a borrowed white, clutch-style evening bag, and Mom's white gloves, remnants from Easters-past. In the 1960s and into the early '70s, women routinely wore hats and gloves to church and on other formal occasions. The gloves from those years remained in Mom's dresser drawer.

The dress took a blue ribbon, but I don't recall it achieving anything more. I think there were two of us in the evening gown class. No silver tray, I can tell you that. I likely would excuse myself to go polish it now, had I won such an award.

But the real mission for that formal remained ahead; the junior prom loomed three seasons away.

FALL AND WINTER CAME and went but still—no boyfriend. We were staring spring in the face, the prom coming in April. I had the dress, but no date. I ended up going to the shindig with my best friend's boyfriend's best friend.

A handsome and nice fella, he went to a different school in a neighboring district. We barely knew each other and never went out again after the prom. Did I feel like a princess at the ball? Not really. If nothing else, this first prom became a lesson in expectations and the danger of giving them too much significance. I know Mom wanted to hear all the glowing details the next day, but there weren't many to tell. I bet she was disappointed.

Yet hope springs eternal, and it wasn't long before I went to work on a second 4-H formal to likewise wear to the senior prom—if, once again, I could possibly land either a boyfriend or a date.

This time, the fabric consisted of a grass-green floral print with a coordinating lining. From the waist down, the dress worked but the bodice disappointed. Mom and I came up with a pattern alteration featuring then-popular cap sleeves, a high neckline, and fabric-covered buttons down the front. I added a bit of lace around the collar and sleeves.

When I wore it that same summer representing my 4-H club in the queen contest (where I didn't win, place, or show), an adult family friend remarked that the gown wasn't flattering. A tough thing to hear, but rather than getting mad, I had to silently agree.

I somehow got a blue ribbon in the dress review, no silver tray again, but surprise—a state-fair sticker in the garment-construction category. The sticker may have been a kindness for all the work (not to mention stress) that goes into creating an evening gown. But it even took a blue ribbon at the Indiana State Fair, which I found satisfying when I viewed the formal on display in our state capital. I would go on to wear the dress to the senior prom but I don't think my date and I ever went out after that.

WITH PROM AND 4-H fair days at last complete, the green gown joined the blue one inside the back of the closet. I had no plans to wear them again, yet a few years later, I came up with some *new* plans for those dresses; long-term ones. Growing up in a household with a huge box full of old clothes that were saved for buttons, lace, zippers, or fabric to recycle in one fashion or another (such as for that third-grade Barbie dress), I pulled these out frequently as a young girl for playing dress-up. They became the wardrobe for variety shows my nieces and I put on for the neighbor kids.

While the prom years found me far too old for such play, I envisioned my formal gowns as being great for future daughters to enjoy as their playtime attire. The dresses were saved over the next several decades, shuffled from one storage closet to another, wherever we lived.

My prom clothing and wedding dress were eventually placed inside a plastic tub, destined for deep storage. Some may gasp at the idea that I didn't have my bridal gown archived in acid-free material and beautifully preserved for someone else to possibly wear later.

I had paid thirty-five dollars for the white dress at a city outlet store. It had the simple lines not so different from earlier prom dresses. I imagine that buttons alone on another bride's gown cost more than my entire ensemble, including veil and accessories.

Even though I have a long, happy marriage, and get attached to many things, not so with my wedding gown. As with the prom dresses, the bridal gown became destined for playtime activities for the next generation of little girls. The future play clothes were stacking up.

I planned to someday fill Mom's cedar chest with the formals, then add all kinds of garage-sale costume jewelry. The girls would love it!

But a funny thing happened on the way to the next generation's playtime. I never had little girls. Instead of Emily and Ellen, God knew that I needed two little boys named Sam and Ben.

The plastic container filled with the old formals became one of the first I went through during that summer of attic organization. When I opened it up to look over these frothy gowns, saved for forty-some years, things didn't appear as I had imagined. The princess-like memories I hoped to see future girls make through these old dresses suddenly evaporated.

The feather trim surrounding the neckline and sleeves of the blue gown appeared in a matted, droopy state. The green-print formal's unflattering style had not improved with age, and felt somehow strange to the touch.

The wedding gown had not fared well either, and the buttons, which I thought might be salvaged as keepsakes, had yellowed along with the rest of the outfit. Not a good look. Not something that anyone appreciated nor treasured wearing, even for playtime.

A little girl playing dress up these days would likely prefer modern, princess-styled dresses from popular entertainment icons instead of these outdated and time-worn relics from the 1970s. And, the old ones wouldn't even fit her.

I could let go of these old gowns and never look back. Some things improve with age, or even if they don't, the years only make them dearer. Other things deteriorate over time. They stay around too long for no good reason.

It's good to know the difference.

7

Clothes call

MOSTLY WHEN I PURCHASE clothes, these days my goal is to find something that makes me think: *Meh. It fits. It doesn't make me look as bad as some other things out there.*

On rare occasions, I spot a top or skirt that's a surprise: a perfect match for an imperfect body. Then I wonder where it's been all my life. I can't believe my good fortune with such a find—something stylish that fits and feels great—that shows mercy even when the scales don't.

Finding clothing I love has nothing to do with price nor place of purchase. With years come sources: a few favorite mail-order catalogs, and two go-to consignment shops. But that special item still simply happens, similar to when sparks fly between two surprising lovebirds, leaving friends to wonder how or where they found one another.

This is the case with my favorite clothing item from the teenage years. Autumn of high school freshman year, the ribbed, navy-blue sweater arrived into my life from a rummage sale. I think it's at the root of my comfort with secondhand clothing.

Mom spoiled me with love and time, but not with lots of new, store-bought clothes. She picked up that medium-weight, V-neck sweater on a rummage table in the little, country community of Brownsville, a few miles from our farm. It probably cost all of a dime in the early 1970s. She culled it from the other preowned clothing that surely filled tables. I loved it from the start, not giving a hoot where it came from.

It became my utility sweater, pairing nicely with bell-bottom jeans or a dressier outfit of a short skirt, hose, and heels. I could wear a button-down shirt underneath and flip up the cuffs, or warm it up during cold, Midwestern winters with an under layer of turtleneck.

It washed and dried like a dream. No grease splatter nor spaghetti-sauce drip had a chance. I wore that sweater so much throughout high school that I finally needed to stop. It likely looked frumpy after so many washings, even as I remained blinded by its inexplicable appeal.

SENIOR YEAR I WORKED nights and weekends in a nice department store, and for the first time, had consistent resources for fashionable, new clothes. Even as my wardrobe expanded, I couldn't bring myself to toss the well-worn sweater. I saved it with what became other favorites in a container of memory clothes.

A flouncy, puffy-sleeved dress joined the sweater. In a blue-and-pink floral pattern, the high-waisted dress made me feel pretty. I wore it to deliver newspaper tear sheets to advertisers the summer following high school. For a short while, I worked in a daily newspaper's advertising department doing odd jobs.

From my work station, I viewed the news desks and even passed by them several times a day. But the two departments remained worlds apart. Then came unexpected layoffs; I found myself hired and let go in the same summer. My dream of being discovered as a budding reporter while working as an office gofer wasn't to be. Besides, that probably only happens in the movies. I needed a journalism degree and then make it to a newsroom somewhere the hard way.

Into that memory-clothes container also went an off-white, smocked-bodice sundress. Spring of senior year I spotted it on display in a popular clothing store that specialized in junior sizes and styles. I told Mom if she bought the dress for me to wear under my graduation gown, that could be my gift for the occasion with nothing else needed. She took me up on the proposal. I wore it for another couple years besides.

I can't forget the yellow, calico sundress. Mom sewed that one late in the summer before high school junior year, designed from memory of a young news reporter who wore a similar outfit.

In those few moments of watching her cover a 4-H dog show, something came to me as though a bolt from heaven. I knew a thing one minute that I had not known the minute before: I wanted to be a newspaper reporter. I wanted to wear cute sundresses on summer days, take photos of, and write stories about, people and communities. I wanted it with everything in me.

Surprisingly, I didn't save the calico dress, so symbolic of that defining moment of my hoped-for career.

ON A SUMMER'S MORNING, decades after packing away the sweater and other miscellaneous, special clothes, we had an unexpected reunion. For all those previous years, I had piled these clothing keepsakes into a container which resided inside our attic. I pulled each folded piece out from layers, an archaeologist unearthing information about eras of my life, told through textile samples. I thought of all that the clothes meant to me as a teenager and young woman, and why certain ones were saved, yet not others that I fondly recall.

Unlike many keepsakes I went through, these weren't even "clothes calls" (or close ones) about what to save. I no longer needed to keep these remnants of eras long gone. I took a few minutes to think about what I wore when special dreams were forming. I thought of when I didn't know how to get from going unnoticed as a newspaper advertising clerk to becoming a career journalist.

Yet life moves forward at an ever-faster pace, and now, I'm retired after the career I wanted and lived out.

No matter how beautiful we think a particular dress is at the time, or a sweater paired with bell bottoms, styles change. *We change.* New life eras emerge. A career turns into retirement—a whole new territory to navigate with its own challenges and expectations.

We learn it's not the clothes we wear that count, but the experiences we have while wearing them. It's the people we are on the inside, not what we look like on the outside.

Those old clothes are gone now, yet a trip inside my bedroom closet reveals a few much more current clothing-memorabilia items. Keeping clothes in other than current sizes isn't recommended in decluttering protocols, yet there they are.

Folded deep on a shelf out of sight is a pair of jeans from my heaviest weight ever, and hanging in the back of my closet is a pair of dress slacks and a dress from my lowest adult weight. Of course, I never want to fit into those jeans again, but doubt that I will ever wear that smallest size, either.

The clothes are reminders of my highs and lows on the scales. I should let them go. Well, *maybe* except for those skinny-clothes items. One always likes to believe anything is possible.

8

Here's hoping

I DON'T REMEMBER HOW I became interested in my mother's cedar-lined hope chest, yet by high school senior year, it had taken residence at the foot of my bed, a white, four-poster canopy number dressed in powder blue. Grandma Jobe had purchased the French Provincial bedroom set for me when she moved in with us years earlier.

I must have spotted the wooden chest in storage inside our barn and asked about it, but regardless how it happened upon my radar, the 1930s, four-legged storage box became mine.

Dad bought it for Mom when they were young, probably engaged, maybe newlyweds. As with so many of our parents' belongings that we wonder about now, the details are missing, and there's no one to ask who knows.

A side note for those blessed to still have their parents and grandparents: ask lots of questions about their lives, beliefs, and belongings. The time will come when you'll want to know and no

43

one will be left to fill in the blanks. It's quite startling one day when you realize that is so.

I don't imagine in Mom's family of origin, that her parents provided cedar-lined hope chests to five daughters during the Great Depression on the income of a homemaker and streetcar conductor. So, I speculate: maybe Mom had always wanted one, so her doting beau or new husband bought it for her as a gift.

Once the chest found its way into my bedroom, into it went things I "hoped" to take into marriage one day, as tradition dictates. First went the olive-green relish dish. Years earlier, in grade school, friend Cheryl and I had bought mismatched, inexpensive dishes at the former Ayr-Way store, dreaming of using them in our future marriages. Years later, I also stashed inside a blue, handmade, crocheted throw.

As I write this, forty-some years after those days, on a chilly winter's night, Brian is using it. It's the one thing that continues to be of practical service from inside that vintage piece of furniture.

I don't know about the interest in hope chests today, but it's a safe bet that they are not at the top of many—any?—young women's wish lists. I wonder if young women these days know what they are; perhaps they have never even heard of them. Have they ever been featured on any popular, home-decorating TV show?

THE CONCEPT OF A hope chest dates much further back than the 1930s when my parents were married, I suspect. The origins point to the ancient tradition of a "dowry," or property in some form that a family gifts to a couple at the launch of their married lives.

In modern terms, it's not so different from a check inside a greeting card presented at the wedding reception, or delivery of a new appliance to the newly married couple's home as a wedding gift.

It could also be, in some families or cultures, a herd of livestock.

Or, as my friend John's great-grandparents provided for his grandparents, a newly built house. The humble home remained in his family for two generations before John proudly assumed the deed.

Cedar chests were places where girls traditionally stored their handiwork such as embroidered samplers, pretty linens, dishes, and silverware. These were accumulated in the years prior to marriage. Tucked away inside the chest, these items remained new and clean as a young woman anticipated the arrival into her life of Mr. Right.

AFTER BRIAN AND I married, we took the chest with us to our first residence, a two-bedroom mobile home. The piece sat in front of our bedroom window. Its contents that related to our newlyweds' home were dispatched throughout the rooms, but I kept inside several youthful keepsakes such as scrapbooks. Even then, I enjoyed memory items from the past.

Being forty-five-years old at the time of our wedding, the chest could use some restoration. The following summer, Brian had time off from teaching high school and said that sure, he's happy to restore this piece of furniture. He wanted to please his new bride— and that bride applauded his suggestion.

For a while that hot summer, I'd drive home from work for lunch, and there he'd be, bless his heart, outside, scraping or sanding away on the old cedar chest.

This labor of love seemed to go on for some time, yet oddly, no measurable progress appeared evident. I guessed this must be more difficult work than I knew. Or perhaps it took lots of time to achieve the meticulous result he was going for.

It took Michelangelo four years to paint the Sistine Chapel ceiling. This chest would be completed much sooner than that. *Maybe.*

Finally, Brian decided to come clean. He admitted that he didn't like this job *at all*, he could never be a woodworker, and the reason it took him so long, with no finish line in sight, is because the only time he could tolerate working on it were the moments he knew I'd be arriving home.

He wanted to please me, but this is his first, and probably last, refinishing project ever, he informed me.

Several lunch hours later, he completed the job. To date, no more work on the chest has been done by either of us. One leg remains detached from the piece, but as long as it sits full of goods, the pressure keeps it in place. It's full of goods.

Despite the chest's old-fashioned looks, it always surprises me when people see it and robustly remark that it's beautiful.

True to Brian's prediction, there have been no additional woodworking projects around our home. We still have a running gag about how one of these days in retirement, we'll hang a wooden shingle outside our home that reads, "Brian's Woodshop."

He isn't too excited about that idea; that joke is getting a little old. As are we.

THE CHEST HAS MOVED with us into every home we've lived in since our marriage. It's been a coffee table, TV cabinet, and currently is the base for a stereo system in our upstairs study. Inside, small keepsakes remain stored. It has housed old scrapbooks, Barbie dolls, and other things we want to keep but don't know where. It's a handy, default storage unit.

Through the years, the box has held two Vietnamese dolls gifted from my brother, Tim, from his tour in Vietnam while serving with the U.S. Navy Seabees during the war.

It also housed the wooden boomerang Tim brought back from Australia when he took an R & R there during those years. He brought our nephew and nieces boomerangs, too, and I well recall how the family gathered in our yard and threw them around.

We waited patiently for those Australian boomerangs to do their thing and return to us. We had understood they were supposed to cooperate, but they never did. They landed instead on the grass or in the barn lot with thumps until we dutifully chased them down.

Decades later, I learned that souvenir boomerangs *do not* work. I'm a little disappointed that we didn't know that then, and wasted time fooling with them.

The chest is a great place to keep childhood trophies and early 4-H sewing projects, including the apron and triangle scarf from that first year. And we can't forget the stored Mary Poppins-themed elementary school lunch box. It's filled with dried corsages from past special occasions.

Who knew that conditions were favorable inside metal lunch boxes for keeping decades-old flowers in more-or-less pristine condition? I know. Some of you beg the question, "Why?" To that I would respond, "Why not?"

WE ALSO ENDED UP with Brian's mother's hope chest. Whereas I took custody of my mom's chest as a teen, Mary's remained in her home until after her passing when eventually Ray's and her belongings were dispersed.

It remains inside our bedroom where, as with the other one, is topped with a stereo system—this one from 1976, a now-vintage setup Brian uses regularly.

One day, probably under the influence of TV decorating shows, I felt frustrated, as though the show-home police were planning to arrive shortly to evaluate our furnishings. I said our bedroom looks like a used-furniture store—one wall filled end-to-end with belongings.

Brian seemed shocked when I proposed getting rid of one of the chests, and by the way, how did he feel about his mom's? Not unexpectedly, he wants to keep it.

I said I'd sacrifice my mother's chest, and replace it upstairs with his mother's piece. Therefore, we were to move one down the stairs and out, and one up the stairs and in.

Huh?

Such a move would mean a lot of work in finding a new storage space for all that stuff in Mom's chest, and we'd need something to hold one of Brian's treasured stereo systems. He likes the way we have it now. He likes it a lot. And remember, we found a way to give each other mutual say about what we keep and what goes, with no fussing nor negotiations involved.

Those home-decorating experts, with their perfectly staged, neutral-hued furnishings, and their lack of sentimental, generational belongings are, to quote a favorite childhood line, "not the boss of me."

WHEN YOU ARE SOLIDLY into your sixties, there are many more considerations than there used to be before shuffling furniture to other parts of one's home—particularly if steps are involved. There are things such as hips and knees that now take priority.

If nothing else, the point of this chapter is this: we're keeping the chests.

We've always said we've got one more home left in us before our final destination. If that's true and we move, some substantial downsizing is required. I'm guessing when the time comes, a pair of 1930s-'40s wooden cedar chests will need to go.

We're past the years in doing the heavy lifting in moving other people's belongings, ours, or those of our kids. At one time, we toted furniture from house to house, and room to room, as though each piece were no heavier than a sack of potatoes.

In my younger years, I might take a notion on a random evening to unload bookshelves and move a set of bookcases to the other side of the room, then reload them immediately. If I didn't like how it looked, I might reverse the process before calling it a night. How

I had that level of energy and drive, I don't know. Those days are history.

We have lots of big, heavy furniture, much of it oak. Brian's brother, Steve, has helped us move several times. He once famously said, "Moving you is like moving Stonehenge. Why couldn't you collect candlesticks?"

We have some of those.

For now, it doesn't look as though we'll be moving those cedar chests or ourselves anywhere. You might say the topics are tabled.

We have some of those, too.

9

Their best advice

WE REMEMBER OUR PARENTS and other loved ones through the objects they leave behind; but even more, through what's stored about them inside our hearts and minds. They were our first teachers and for many of us, also our greatest influencers regarding life, and how to live it.

These stories—my parents' best advice—continue to serve me well.

As a girl of thirteen, I wanted to learn how to drive Dad's smaller farm tractor. Why not? Boys my age drove tractors, and, it would be three whole years before I'd get behind the wheel of an automobile—an eternity when you're that age.

Driving a tractor is different from steering a car. I could learn how and roll immediately, no license required. If the world wasn't my oyster, our Indiana farm was, and I could almost feel the wind blowing back my hair as I imagined tooling around fields and pastures on breezy, summer evenings—doing *what* exactly, I didn't know—but driving nonetheless.

Mom never drove a tractor, but made her share of trips to town in the family car to locate parts for a broken one, usually in crunch-time situations with a crop being planted or a harvest under way; time of the utmost importance.

She must have heard me campaigning to Dad on this topic of tractor-driving, but didn't have anything to offer while I spoke with him about it. I vividly recall the living room setting where I received her advice. Dad had just left the house. It appeared that Mom had waited for precisely the right moment to share her viewpoint to this audience of one, delivered in her calm, quiet voice.

"If I were you," she confided, "I wouldn't learn to drive the tractor."

"Why not?" I asked, puzzled.

"If you do, your dad will expect you to become a farmhand," she said simply. "One day you'll be sixteen, and wanting to go on a date or out with your friends, and instead he'll have you plowing the fields."

Oh. I hadn't thought of it that way, yet instantly knew how my strong-willed father operated. So did Mom. Dad would be equal-opportunity about farm work, not discriminating against his girl in the least if I had the qualifications to do the job, let alone the interest. My electrician brothers hadn't wanted to become farmers, but maybe Dad would make one out of his daughter, he may have thought.

Sure, driving the tractor seemed a fun lark then, but that's all I had in mind. I had dreams for my teen years. Farming didn't make the list.

After hearing Mom's advice, I steered clear of asking again about driving the tractor, and Dad didn't offer to teach me. Since I had been so adamant in asking him to show me the ropes, I imagine that I wasn't the only one who landed a private conference with Mom.

My mother's advice concerned more than literal farm tractors. I have thought of the tractor story many times in a variety of life situations. More than once, I've been complimented by friends for an ability to decline when asked to take on something I didn't want to do.

It's always been a simple decision because I frame it this way: Is what they're offering, metaphorically, a tractor that I want to drive? And if it is, do I want to plow the fields later? I count the cost of what will be expected down the road—country or otherwise.

If a boss needs a volunteer for a project, do I want to step up? Sounds great, being a helpful, above-and-beyond employee and all, but volunteering once might mean the project becomes mine going forward.

AN INDEPENDENT, CRUSTY FARMER, Dad saw things as his way or the highway. I arrived many years after my folks' two older sons were born. Our family had a unique dynamic regarding the spacing of children; almost as though my parents had three separate families, even though we had the same parents.

Dad once said he wouldn't know what to do with a daughter in the house. Yet he found out quickly after my arrival. In younger years, I enjoyed being Daddy's girl, tagging along around the barnyard, becoming his assistant with the farm animals, and delighting in his teaching me how to swim in our pond, ride a pony, and roller skate.

My father loved to skate, perfecting the skill during years of transporting school-bus loads of kids to school-sponsored outings at the rink. Due to his one-on-one skating lessons, a point of pride for me in junior high became these evenings. During school skates, the principal always found me because of my old-fashioned skating skills. While other girls skated with their boyfriends, I skated with Mr. Cummins!

Born long after Mom had birthed two sons and experienced a miscarriage, I came as both a surprise and as her last shot at a daughter, in the weeks before she turned forty-five. Although a tomboy, which pleased my father, I also managed to be a girly-girl who loved to dress up, play with dolls, and pursue traditional home-and-family arts, which delighted my mother.

Both gave me the best that traditional farm life could offer: acres to roam for picking morel mushrooms in the spring; playing in a grove where my best friend and I imagined a tree-trunk playhouse; a farm pond to swim in all summer long; ponies and later a horse to ride.

DAD TAUGHT ME THE meaning of "getting back on the horse" when you fall off. My pony, Ginger, used a successful technique to toss me by trotting around the pasture, sweet as sugar, then abruptly throwing her head down so I'd tumble over the top.

Onto the ground I'd land, scared, angry, and tearful. Dad calmly watched the incident occur repeatedly, unmoved by my tears, each time instructing me to, "Get back on."

Despite my tears and complaints, the ornery pony threw me again and again, until I learned how to ride out her antics. Finally, we made our peace and she gave up tossing me.

What a life lesson: getting back on the horse; riding out the bad times. How often does life throw us? We may find ourselves reduced to tears, and wonder how we'll possibly find the courage to get up and try again. Yet we do.

FROM DAD CAME OLD stories of his years as a basketball player for a small high school. Enthralled by his tales, I spent many evenings with him discussing the specifics of certain games, and how his father got recruited for a job in another town—complete with a job offer—all because they wanted Dad on their basketball roster. Or so the story goes. The family stayed put. The notion of moving away seemed to them akin to treason.

I don't know that anyone else, Mom included, ever listened in such detail to my father's glory-days stories as I did. I treasured hearing them repeated as much as Dad delighted in telling them.

My parents attended basketball games supporting my high school, and we discussed those inside and out afterwards, evaluating the players, the plays, the questionable calls, the outcomes, the outlook for the week ahead, and always, for the sectional tournament that loomed large at season's end.

One year, as I babysat neighbor kids in their home, I read in the newspaper that our high school basketball team would play in a holiday tournament one year from then. It would be at a large, area high school, with a noted Indianapolis school participating. Overcome with anticipation—a full year out—I called Dad to talk about this new development.

"I wish we didn't have to wait a whole year for that game!" I complained. "I wish we could skip forward twelve months and play that game right now!"

Dad's calm advice surprised me. "Don't wish your life away," he said. At about age sixty at the time, he could no doubt see the speed at which his own life passed by, the same way I see mine galloping onward now.

Since that night, often I've been elated anticipating a future happening, and didn't know how I could *possibly* endure the wait. But then I'll remember my father's advice, and realize how right he had been.

We need to treasure each day and its offerings, delights, and challenges. Tomorrow will get here—and be gone—soon enough.

WHILE MOM TAUGHT WHAT *not* to do through the tractor story, she told me what *to* do in two areas of life that I use daily.

As an eighth grader, while I contemplated registration for freshman courses, Mom strongly advised that I take typing class.

She knew I could use the skill throughout life, and it would open doors in, at minimum, office work of various kinds. It hadn't been in my plans but I took her at her word, and felt grateful for the idea.

It became a blessing to learn how to type during first semester of freshman year, then follow up with the advanced class as a sophomore. I joined the school newspaper staff, and by senior year, became editor.

Clerical work followed after graduation, and as a young-married woman, I worked full-time in an office while pursuing my journalism degree at night. Meanwhile, Brian taught days and worked on his advanced-education degree on the side.

Rare is the day since I learned to type that I haven't written on a keyboard.

I inherited my mother's old typewriter. Prohibitive to even lift due to its considerable weight, the machine's keys served as a workout for the fingers. I kept it for many years as a conversation piece, finally discarding it as it wasn't worth its weight in shelf space and dust, and with modern technology, there's no use for it.

BUT WHEN IT COMES to the best advice I ever received, there's my mother's example. A quiet woman, she lived out her faith more than she discussed it. A dedicated Christ follower, she wanted the same for me and for our family members, as I want for mine today.

I believed in God, but didn't get serious about a personal relationship with Jesus until my middle twenties. At that time, the Holy Spirit pursued me. I found a church home, and set out on a quest to have a dedicated walk with the Lord. It's a lifelong journey.

Recently I found something while going through some reclaimed books that Mom had borrowed from me long ago. Why had I never before noticed in one of them these words, in my late mother's handwriting? Written on one of the books I found this:

"Believe in God. It is true—to Donna. Ask God to receive Him."

I looked at when that book had printed: 1983. The middle 1980s are when I felt drawn to faith in Jesus in a new, highly personal way. My faith blossomed during that period, and continues to sustain me, as I pray it always will. I don't know when my mom wrote that on the book she borrowed from me, but I know of her deep desire, and that she felt concerned for my spiritual welfare.

Never underestimate the significance of a mother's prayers for her children. This scripture comes to mind:

Direct your children onto the right path, and when they are older, they will not leave it.

— Proverbs 22:6 (NLT)

AS YOU CONSIDER YOUR best advice either received or given to others, keep in mind that my folks never had a thought that when they offered these gems, their comments would remain on my mind and inside my heart during all my days.

Guard and measure your words as you share them with others, and remember that people are always listening, and what sticks with them might be comments that you had no idea carried so much weight. Fifty or seventy years from now, your loved ones may still be quoting you. Make what you say—or what you wisely don't say—count.

10

A folder full of no

I HAD FORGOTTEN ABOUT the white folder and its contents until it appeared, sitting atop Brian's old school papers inside a large, plastic container. I have no memory of how the folder got there, but can guess that we added it two moves ago. Likely, we were in a rush to get everything packed while not wasting available space, and into the tub it went.

On front is handwritten in blue ink, "Rejection letters," with a big, hastily-drawn frowny face in the righthand corner. Inside the folder are about a dozen such letters, mostly from the 1980s.

I believe the folder started with a college magazine-writing course. Either the instructor or maybe a guest speaker suggested it, telling the budding journalists that we should save the rejection letters we receive from our submissions.

Oh, we'd be rejected plenty, we were told. We can expect that before we get a glimmer of yes, there will be many answers of no. "Enough to paper a wall," is the phrase that rings in my mind.

Why I thought that saving publication rejections and papering a wall with them might prove inspirational, I'll never know. Maybe it became my way of laughing off defeat and disappointment by mocking them in this strange way.

Yet reading those letters these many years later is not a humorous exercise, but a queasy one. More than the specific rejections, what's bothersome is recognizing the inadequacy of my submissions. Those ranged from personal essays to overly researched women's issues. I would have been shocked had anyone ever accepted my work. I aimed too high. Wincing now, I recognize my audacity in sending those submissions to national magazines.

Rejections arrived in the form of one-size-fits-all postcards, while others were letters either trying to let me down easy and end on a pleasant note, or let me down hard and thank me anyway.

I kept them all, letting them stack inside the folder—not enough to paper a wall, but for a while, that option looked more promising than did publication.

IN MAGAZINE-WRITING CLASS, OUR assignments were built around various writing prompts. We learned to pen query letters to periodicals that might be good fits for our themes, and what to expect from the editors who read them.

Our instructor gave us an interesting, if unlikely, challenge. He said that anyone who gets a magazine submission published during the semester receives an automatic A in the class.

I rolled out yet another query, this one to *TIME* magazine, a letter to the editor. Not exactly a well-researched, thought-provoking piece with a large word count. This round, however, when the postcard arrived, it came with a twist: my submission had been accepted, set to appear in an upcoming issue!

The class instructor seemed impressed. True to his word, when I produced the evidence inside the printed magazine with my name attached, I got an A for the course. And no. In case you're wondering, one is not paid for letters to the editor. I never made anything close to a living in freelance writing. I dare say for most freelancers, other than an elite few, such work is probably more hobby or side hustle than consistent income; certainly, at the level I know it. Yet for those who enjoy freelancing, it can be a one aspect of a writing career.

I placed a few pieces, but as life became busier with our children in school, I stopped submitting things elsewhere and concentrated on my newspaper day job. While I had known since my teens that I wanted to work at a paper to earn my bread and butter, I considered magazine writing the dessert.

I GREW UP READING various magazines that entered our home, especially Mom's homemaking monthlies. I inhaled the feature pieces in a weekly TV publication about the "real lives" of my favorite television stars.

I kept a stack of choice magazine issues, a few dating to the early 1980s, and occasionally find inspiration in projects and ideas on those pages that I bookmarked for *someday* when more time arrived. These magazines look and feel oddly thick by today's standards. The publications are pre-internet, from a time when a monthly periodical might seem dense as a novel.

But even if I had connections and talent for a full-time magazine career, which I probably didn't, it wouldn't have happened. Family life required much of me from the late 1980s through the 2000s. The years were packed with raising our sons and with concerns for elderly parents, along with managing the home front while Brian handled a demanding career as the family's primary breadwinner.

My steady newspaper work and home life were plenty on my plate, and I remain grateful for those thirty-one years with one employer. By retirement, I had spent half my life working for the same publication. I wrote about World War II veterans, artisans and artists, overcomers, people with unique tales to tell, and those special God moments that give us goosebumps. I felt humbled with the responsibility of telling people's most treasured or harrowing stories.

It's interesting how sometimes in life when we least expect it, we're granted the unique desires of our hearts. I see such graces ultimately as gifts from above.

One day while minding my own business at my newspaper desk, probably typing into a calendar the listings for upcoming events or club news, Tina, our newspaper publisher, came by my desk, paused briefly, and said, "I'm starting a women's magazine. I want you to be the editor."

For nine-and-a-half years, I had the privilege of steering this local quarterly publication, making editorial decisions about themes and covers, columnists, and reader giveaways.

I'll always be grateful to Tina, to the community that supported and looked forward to those issues, and most especially to the good Lord for providing that special dessert as a part of my writing career.

There are only so many specific job openings out there. But time and again I've seen that we can get a taste of those big dreams on small scales. And they might even be just as sweet—at least in their own way—or in ways we'd never considered possible.

WHILE GOING THROUGH THE attic, I found a couple more rejection letters. One is from a large amusement park I enjoyed visiting with my best friend back in the day. We loved riding roller coasters so much that we wrote a letter to the park asking if we might attempt breaking a record for the longest streak of continuously riding a coaster.

Park management wasn't interested in hosting us; the park already held the record and had nothing to gain by accommodating us.

And then there's the other one. My high school senior year, I sent a letter and resume to our community's weekly newspaper, asking for a job. I had enjoyed this newspaper regularly since childhood. The general manager seemed to do about everything around the paper. I read later that he ended up being affiliated with the publication for half a century. I anticipated the rejection (which came), but asked anyway.

Sometimes we figure that the no is coming, but we still try. Life is always a balance in that way between hitting on a surprise yes, and getting the no we dread. I've had both, along with a few maybes.

I'm throwing away the rejection letters.

Paper a wall with them? Um, that's a wall full of no.

11

Thinking inside the box

YOU'LL NEVER DESCRIBE BRIAN and me as hip and trendy. Those terms aren't in our genes, and our jeans aren't particularly fashionable, either. We tend to hold onto objects as long as there's a smidgen of use remaining.

It should come as no surprise that when flat-screen, high-definition TVs became the norm, we went right on using our old-style, box television sets because they still worked fine. And by the way, does anyone still add the word "set" to the word "television?" Apparently I do.

Gradually, the sets gave out, and one by one, we upgraded. At last, the old TVs had been replaced in the living room, study, and bedroom. A small kitchen model quietly held its ground in the corner of our countertop, as it had for twenty-two years. I kept waiting, and waiting, and waiting some more for it to bite the dust.

I decided to make a bold request of Brian: "If the kids want to know what I want for Christmas, I wouldn't mind replacing the kitchen set with a flat screen."

In a break with family precedent, I received the smart set on Christmas day. The non-smart version got a demotion to the garage work bench.

"Hate to throw it out," Brian said. Son Ben added, "You should hook it up." Gene pools run deep.

As for the smart TV, new cable hook-up equipment is required. Smart televisions are fancy that way. They are, after all, *smart*. They aren't compatible with the old, ignorant stuff.

We used the occasion of a trip to the cable company to round up all the stray remote controls and assorted cords associated with televisions-past—as well as mysterious wires for who knows what, TVs or not. Maybe the cable people will know what they're for. Brian packaged them up nicely inside a sturdy, lidded shoebox.

He waited in the parking lot while I went inside to do business. Along with retrieving the new set's gadgetry, I presented the box of the old stuff to our provider, with our compliments.

The cable guy glanced at our box of wires and plugs and apparently found it useless; no further examination needed. My first clue? He calmly (and instantly) said, "If you don't want all this, we can dispose of it."

Oh. Okay. That works.

I thought Brian would celebrate the news. Instead, his words when I returned to the car were, "They kept the box? That's a good box. You should have gotten that back."

It can only be explained as a senior moment that I didn't.

CHRISTMAS DAY FINDS ME waiting for gift recipients to hurry and open their presents so that it may be asked if they intend to keep their boxes. It's polite to inquire before pouncing and grabbing, right? And if they aren't going to reuse that bow … may I?

At the newspaper, copier paper arrives in wonderful, sturdy boxes, complete with lids. Sometimes they save a few empties for storing file papers, but mostly, it's open season on the spares.

Maybe one needs to be of a certain age before truly appreciating the merits of an outstanding box. A box with a sturdy lid? Be still my heart.

I'm not alone. Certainly not in my own household. Brian and I had been so busy rescuing *good* boxes, then tossing them into the attic for safe keeping, that when we finally ventured into the attic, it seemed as though instead, we had entered a shipping warehouse.

"We need to get rid of those boxes," Brian finally said after navigating the maze.

"Not that one, though," I cautioned, pointing out a particularly perfect specimen. "That's a very good box. Oh, and don't even think about tossing those with the lids. Those are hard to come by."

It used to be when you bought something at a nice department store, clerks routinely asked if you needed a gift box and were happy to tuck a lovely one, complete sometimes with tissue paper, into your package.

"Would you like a handled shopping bag? You've got your hands full," they might sweetly add.

"Why, yes; yes I would. Thank you," I might respond.

Then times changed as they tend to do. Ask for a box today and if that option is even available, you're likely sent on a hike: "You'll need to go to the service desk. It's in the far-righthand back corner."

I OFTEN ACCEPTED OFFERS for complimentary retail boxes because I figured the gravy train would end one day. I planned to be ready with my private stash of gently used department-store specimens.

My favorite of those department stores is no longer in business. I'd say, "I told you so," if it weren't so sad. I hope the free boxes weren't their undoing. I could have bailed them out with a trip to our attic.

Now with all the shipping boxes that arrive at people's doors due to online shopping, I'm looking ahead and seeing the possibility of a day when we'll all be charged a box fee along with our trash-collection bill. It may be here by the time you're reading this book.

During the pandemic, there were so many home-delivered cardboard boxes placed in people's trash that it became a topic at the local-government level in at least one community I know. The gathering and disposing of all that extra cardboard had become a municipal issue.

But don't despair. Some of us will keep doing our part. If you see someone of a certain age—say, mine—watching you intensely when you open a package, don't worry. They're perfectly harmless and wouldn't think of swiping your goods.

It's the box they're after.

And the bow, if it's nice.

12

Speaking of boxes

THE INQUIRY TOOK ME by surprise. My librarian sister-in-law, Linda, asked if I might give a program to patrons about Christmas gift-wrap ideas. She said I'd always been good at wrapping presents. Would I share some techniques?

Flattered by both the compliment and the offer, I got busy assembling a program. As I gathered and embellished sample boxes, the irony made me chuckle.

Senior year of high school, I worked part time as a fitting-room monitor in a nice department store. There, I sat inside the dressing-room doorway, counting the number of clothing items carried inside, then assigning small hangers to shoppers, designating that number. The process reversed when shoppers left the stalls.

Boring work, but when I cashed the paychecks, which translated into employee-discounted outfits for myself, and nice Christmas gifts for family members, I didn't mind.

When stock arrived in crates, they placed it outside the dressing room where I unpacked and hung the clothing if there were no dressing-room customers. It wasn't long before the monitoring assignment went on the back burner as they transitioned me into a utility employee.

One night I might refill greeting-card slots in the stationery department or collect zippered bags stuffed with money from registers at closing time. Other shifts had me ringing up meal tickets in the upstairs restaurant or weighing bulk candy.

I assisted women with their "foundational" needs in the intimate-apparel department—although I had little idea how to help as my own underthings were uncomplicated. I learned how to work huge, push-button cash registers that growled with every entered price.

ONE BUSY DECEMBER SATURDAY, they sent me to the customer-service department to wrap holiday presents. The seasonal gift paper remained the same for each box: matte red, finished with a strip of green ribbon around the middle, topped with a matching bow. How hard could this be?

"I can't put these out there!" my supervisor bellowed, assessing several of my completed packages. "These are *terribly* wrapped gifts."

They never again requested me to pinch-hit in that department. The memory and embarrassment of the supervisor's harsh criticism seemed to confirm: *I am terrible at wrapping presents.*

Never considering that the supervisor could have been overly critical, her judgment imprinted on my self-esteem. As the years passed, I tried to redeem that memory by adding flair to personal gifts. If a kitchen-shower present is required, I might wrap it in a pretty kitchen towel and top the package with a spatula instead of a bow. I'd wrap a little boy's box with an old road map, then bling it out with a toy car on top.

My specialty became recycling colorful, newspaper-comics pages into wrapping paper, then fashioning bows from strips of the cartoons, folded accordion-style.

I saved boxes, be them department-store versions, or the gold standard—sturdy, lidded envelope boxes recycled from the newspaper office.

Simple techniques were picked up: fold the seams of cut-paper edges under before taping them down. Use the amount of paper you precisely need, eliminating bulk (and waste) on the ends of the package.

I didn't want anyone remarking again about the terrible nature of my skills. But thirty-six years later, being asked to give a *library program?* What a special invite. For weeks, I worked on what to show and tell as I gathered and decorated boxes. The packages could span the length of a library table at the front of the conference room.

I decided that we needed a make-and-take activity. I rifled through a box of ribbons, pictures cut from greeting cards, colorful card stock, markers, and glue—assembling a station for library patrons to create their own gift tags.

We also needed a door prize. That could be the book angel I crafted by folding pages of a thrifted book to create her skirt, adding a foam ball for her head, and a recycled CD halo.

Program day arrived. With happy butterflies in my middle, I stopped to pick up Linda's mother, Lucille, a vibrant woman whose company I always enjoyed. My brother-in-law, Steve, also attended the program.

What I learned from the experience is that I love creating programs. The anticipation about who will show up, and watching the delight people take at the possibility of winning even a small door prize, is addictive.

This also became my secret day of redemption over that supervisor's long-ago insult.

MORE THAN A SINGLE program, the experience prefaced my life's next chapter. I had toyed with the idea of writing a novel, but didn't say much about it. The next year I spent nearly every spare moment finishing it.

Being a self-published author with no name recognition, to sell books, I'd need to make myself available for speaking engagements. What I knew as a newspaper reporter who typed event listings into a calendar, is that most organizations need a steady flow of speakers.

I had an idea of how to give a program, garnered from years of attending presentations—and from my gift-wrap experience. Brian had a simple tip: "No one wants to hear anyone speak about anything for more than twenty minutes." His advice proves legitimate because whenever inquiries come about my program length, a typical response to, "Twenty minutes," is a sigh of relief, along with the word, "Perfect!"

Following the gift-wrap presentation, I squirreled away the wrapped pretend gifts into the attic where they sat for years. Finally, the day arrived to let them go. I no longer needed the boxes that had provided the dress rehearsal for what became regular speaking gigs related to my books.

One program led to the next. It doesn't matter the number of attendees, there is always a blessing involved; one often not measured in book sales. My mantra for a couple hundred book-related programs and opportunities I've been offered, including vendor booths, festivals, and author fairs, is to look for the blessing. It's *always right there*, and often surprising in what it ends up being.

It could be that a former boss I hadn't seen in years hears about the program and shows up. Maybe while standing in line in a gift shop where an author fair takes place, I meet an unexpected kindred spirit who becomes a writing mentor. It could be one of my novels is featured by a book club whose members serve a meal based around recipes inside my book.

It could also be I'm expecting a crowd of twenty and two hundred arrive. Or, that I'm expecting a crowd of two hundred when two people show up, but then we connect so well, none of us want to close our time together.

It's all part of this package called life. And to think: Part of this journey began long ago with a poorly wrapped present. Who could have guessed that present would become a beautiful gift?

13

Let sleeping bags lie

FOR SIXTY YEARS, THE rolled-up sleeping bag mostly stayed that way—coiled in a storage space inside an attic or on a garage shelf. Manufactured before there were lightweight, weather-resistant materials for campers, the bulky bag is inefficient outdoors in the cold—by today's standards, anyway.

The bag's family roots are a bit mysterious. Brian recalls that his dad purchased it long ago from a department store. What stumps the son is why. An avid fisherman whenever he got the chance, Ray never went on overnight trips.

Brian's folks were frugal, as were mine, so there had to be a specific occasion for this purchase of a new sleeping bag, rather than to simply make do with a piece of tarp and a stack of old blankets. Could it be the family expected company and prepared for possible overflow? Maybe someone had suggested an overnight campout.

But lest I slander that sleeping bag because it isn't thoroughly modern, I must admit that it came in pretty handy on a number of occasions through the years. During the period that his folks had custody of the bag, Brian borrowed it for a few years when he chaperoned school kids' overnight trips to a science camp. Son Sam borrowed it on Boy Scout campouts. Son Ben used it once for an out-of-state weekend with friends at a music festival.

Come to think of it, we seemed to need it so frequently that the brown bag with the yellow mallard duck lining remained in a corner of our attic. It had never been washed in all the time we had it, and I have to wonder if it had *ever* seen suds. Probably not. Yet oddly enough, it had no odor nor stains.

THE SLEEPING BAG HIT my radar as one of the first items I had targeted for elimination when the attic project began. I planned to load it up for donation and send it away. In our sixties, Brian and I anticipate little chance of ever roughing it on the hard ground. Oh, who am I kidding? Make that zero chance.

These days, if our adult sons or their future families ever need a sleeping bag, they would likely pick up sleek, insulated ones made with state-of-the-art materials from a favorite sporting-goods store. They would not come home to raid our attic for the old standby. Would they?

Brian thought if we were going to donate the bag, we should at least wash it. Considering that it contains decades' worth of sweat, that seemed only right.

I unrolled the unlikely heirloom, unzipped it, and found myself taken aback with the vibrantly colored flannel lining—all of it perfect and not faded in the least. The bag itself is likewise in nearly pristine condition. The zipper and drawstring exterior allow one to not only roll up, but tie off the bag.

For the fun of it, Brian decided to do an online-marketplace search. We were surprised to find several vintage bags for sale that are exactly like ours. I could envision these unzipped and covering beds in woodsy cabins. Maybe an actual demand exists for these. Does this mean that we should keep it and list it online ourselves? Suddenly, the entrepreneurial genes began to kick in. Donating it had become merely one option.

The sleeping bag had taken over our day. We thought its bulk would overwhelm our washing machine and dryer, so we spontaneously decided to head to the local laundromat and while there, go ahead and wash the heavy bedspread from our bedroom. It needed to be cleaned, anyway.

We went together on a nice summer's Saturday afternoon, the only humans in the business establishment the whole time we were there.

As the sleeping bag and bedspread swirled and spun inside separate machines, we joked around and talked, sharing old family stories and new ideas about this project—an offshoot of my season of attic cleaning. Maybe we should start an online store and sell some of our other finds, we considered.

As the day went on though, and we looked into the idea of becoming online merchants, along with all that's potentially involved with such a thing, we decided we weren't ready to become shopkeepers. We simply wanted our attic cleaned out.

The speculation however, continued about the chocolate-hued sleeping bag, and we laughed at this much concentration of time spent on our find.

Maybe this is the gift of retirement: spontaneous, quality, couple time spent without worrying that we should be occupied with something more practical.

No, we simply enjoyed our hours together hanging out in this most unlikely place for fun, a laundromat—an illustration of the principle that it's not what you're doing or where you're going that matter—it's who you're with.

The bag washed and dried beautifully. Back at home, I unfolded it on the bed with a new appreciation for its craftsmanship, and how well it holds up over time.

I like things that hold up over time.

With the sleeping bag clean, rolled up, and placed on our linen-closet shelf, I wonder how its next assignment will unfold.

We still have no idea what led to the sleeping bag's purchase, but here it is, still serving this family, its story continuing—alongside our own.

14

---❦---

To keep or not to keep?

WHEN I PULLED OUT my father's blue-striped coveralls, I knew they had to go. Dad has been gone thirty years, and the faded-denim work clothes haven't seen the light of day since I folded them away with other memory items decades ago.

For a moment, though, the sight nearly took my breath away; the well-worn clothing had been Dad's self-imposed farm uniform. Held up to their full size, they appeared familiar, almost as though Dad had moments earlier stepped out of them after a day's work. Yet they looked surprisingly small compared to the image I keep of my larger-than-life farmer father.

The clothing hailed from another era; one that can't be duplicated in the present without a specific farm and my particular father on it.

In Dad's experience, the coveralls came out in cooler weather, worn over varying numbers of layers befitting the day's temperatures. When not in use, the outer garment hung in the basement stairwell, not inside a closet nor folded within a drawer. This way no grease, oil, mud, nor other farm-life soil would carry grime throughout the house.

The clothing never added more work to my mother's tidy manner of housekeeping. The coveralls could be removed in the old-time utility basement, then washed if needed, or hung on a nail in the stairwell wall.

When I mentioned to a friend the releasing of these coveralls into the universe, she said I should keep them to recycle the fabric into a teddy bear. A teddy bear? What am I, five? *Maybe; not a bad idea,* I thought. *Or a pillow,* my mind added. Either project would be exactly the *kind* of thing I typically do.

Once upon a time I rescued a worn-out quilt from my parents' basement, and spent months transforming the fan-shaped blocks into hand-sewn decorations stitched onto sweatshirts for all the adult females on that side of the family. I have no idea if any of them actually *liked* or wore the sweatshirts. I know that mine is no longer in my wardrobe.

With that experience in mind, I decided that I have plenty of keepsakes from my father, and didn't need to create a new memory project with the coveralls. If I chose such a venture, I would end up moving the clothing to another storage space. Then the goal of *someday* upcycling it into something else would go onto a long-term to-do list.

That would not be cleaning out, but complicating things. Not what I have in mind.

I mean, why stop with one teddy bear or pillow? Make them for Dad's great-grandkids; even his great-greats. Cut the fabric into strips and wind those around plastic Christmas balls for the tree. Use a piece of coverall fabric inside a picture frame as a mat behind his photo.

Those might be great ideas, but no. I'm not turning this project into a cottage industry.

ONE POTENTIAL STUMBLING BLOCK I find while decluttering is this concept of future projects. Almost everything we no longer want to keep in its present form can be transformed into something else through paint, glue, nails, saws, and the time it takes to pull off such projects.

The to-do-list of ideas combined with the raw material can weigh a person down even further than keeping the original item. Nope. The coveralls were going away.

Even after eliminating numerous containers of keepsakes from our attic, to the casual eye, our home remains full. If one looked deeper, into drawers and cupboards, that same eye might still see the makings of a family museum! That's not what we're after.

We keep many things, yet realize it's impossible to hold onto everything saved by previous generations that comes with a story, a pleasant memory, or an idea for what it *could* become with application of a little elbow grease or a glue gun.

Letting go of things our loved ones held onto, then stored for decades, is not easy, but there is something freeing about making decisions and taking actions that feel correct. Use it or lose it, we've heard. I would add: keep it and love it. But beyond that, show it the door.

I'd say if the decision to retain something hinges on buying more supplies for improving it, think again.

TAKE THE 1930s-ERA occasional chair that belonged to Brian's folks. The chair has skinny, wooden legs and slim armrests. Its small stature contrasts with how much larger many people and homes are in today's society. At first glance, the chair doesn't look like much. Its tufted back is interesting, but the chair in no way screams (nor whispers) comfort.

Maybe if you look up a definition for the term, "occasional chair," you would find this: a nondescript chair that doesn't provide much comfort nor particular notice. It sits out of the way in a home in case the need arises for extra seating.

This particular chair, however, offers a surprise in that it truly is comfortable!

"I always liked that chair," Brian says.

When I host a life group from church in our home, I have found that one member tends to gravitate to it. Once you sit there, you might be hooked.

The chair had a problem, though. The dingy fabric had a stain on the seat. Because an occasional chair isn't necessary for our living room, which already hosts three large recliners and a sectional sofa, the solution in our family would normally be to move the damaged heirloom to the attic and effectively punt on making any long-term decision regarding its fate.

Reupholstering even a small piece of furniture is expensive, equal to the cost of a nice, new one. I know because I priced it.

After we got over the shock of the estimate, we discussed what to do. I said that storing it away in its unusable state should not be an option. Either we reupholster it, or we let it go by donating it to charity, or wish it well on its journey to that great living room in the sky.

We both came down in the middle on this one. I blinked first.

"Let's get it recovered as long as I don't have to hear another word about the price tag involved."

Brian agreed.

I chose an unusual fabric, incorporating colors from the room in a lively, geometric pattern. Now we've got too much money in it to let it go. At the same time, it fits in well, and it's ready for prime time—useful and attractive.

WE DID, HOWEVER, LET the cuckoo clock go. The prompt came from preparing to paint the living room. The clock had not worked in years, even after spending a wad of money sending it off to a specialty repairman. Restored for only a short time, its minutes started slipping. What good is a clock with slippery minutes?

The clock required manual rewinds daily, and then when you forgot, you had to move the fragile hands to the correct time and begin again. Not sustainable.

Over time, we decided not to use it for a timepiece, but left it hanging high enough on the wall for its chains to drop nicely without touching the floor—effectively making it an ornament. The hole in the wall would be a problem if we took down this clock because nothing else would work for its unusually high placement.

This could be our chance to remove the clock and get the hole professionally repaired as part of the new paint job. Or, we could dump more money into it.

The clock had been my favorite belonging of Brian's parents. It came to them from a niece who had been stationed as a U.S. Air Force nurse in Germany. We have no idea if the piece had great or minimal dollar value. Either way, the purchase made for a charming gift that functioned well for decades.

It hung high on my in-laws' kitchen wall. Having grown up in a home with silent clocks, I found the noisy timepiece delightful; the consistent ticking comforting; and the overall features of the brown-painted wooden clock whimsical. Even during the night, in the early days of sleeping over at their house, I sometimes awakened when the clock sounded, then listened to count off the bird's call to learn the hour, and resume a peacefully sweet slumber.

We hoped to keep this household heirloom. But once it no longer worked, even following a pricey repair, we were over it. I told Brian that as expensive as it is to fix, and it still failed to keep working right, there's little point in donating it to charity, only to frustrate someone else with what they would need to spend.

Finally, we made the decision. I pulled off the pinecone weights and a bird decoration. The bird will go on the Christmas tree as a keepsake and the hefty weights will likely join a bowl full of real pinecones during the winter months. (Why is it that we associate pinecones with Christmas or winter?)

WE ALSO DONATED MY mother's portable sewing machine on which I stitched early 4-H projects. But Mom bought a new model a year or two after that and the old workhorse went into the dark recesses of a closet.

Years after Brian and I married, Mom gave me the vintage sewing machine. I even got it overhauled into perfect working order. But the fact remained that I never truly enjoyed sewing and had little talent for it. With the overhaul complete, I attempted a dress.

To my own disappointment, and as much as I *tried* to enjoy machine sewing, I had not changed. I could ignite no real spark of interest, only frustration with the process. And I never liked the finished dress.

While I took sewing for many years in 4-H, my efforts required plenty of answers from pleas of, "Mom! Help!" I sewed because I loved to select patterns, fabric, and enjoyed what we then called dress reviews where we modeled our outfits. Yet aside from these projects, I never machine sewed for pleasure.

I wish I cared about sewing. I truly do, in the same way I wish I cared about calculus. It's a theoretical kind of caring. In practice, not so much. Let's put it this way, if there's a choice between working with fabric, numbers, or words, the words win every time. I'm glad there are those who are proficient in both sewing and calculus. I'm not one of them.

After another forty years of storage in the back of dark closets, I gathered the original owner's manual, slipped it inside the weathered, brown case, and donated the machine.

Keeping and letting go can be complex. Sometimes life is simply hard enough in other ways that we have to make our own swift executive decisions about such things. Then we move on.

15

Pen pals

WHO AMONG US OWNS only one junk drawer? You always hear the term used singularly, as in, "What does that key go to that you keep in the junk drawer?"

The junk drawer? Which one? We have a number of them. Probably one or even two in most every room. I bet you do, too.

Several of these catch-all spaces hold office supplies of every kind—even though in our house, we're often hard-pressed to find a pair of scissors. Maybe they're buried under the writing utensils.

We own many interesting ink pens. There are pencils, but not as many, and these may never see a sharpener since we rarely use lead at our house. A pencil is used on the rare occasion when Brian signs off on a new nail hole in the wall so I can hang something (nothing short of an act of Congress). He doesn't use the pencil to sign legislation on the matter, but rather, to mark the spot on the wall stud.

If he had his way, our walls would remain blank canvases.

Because of his severe dislike for taking a hammer to the wall, it takes considerable negotiation to get one approved. It's okay! What can I tell you? We all have our pet peeves.

All that is to say—use of pencils is that rare.

I'm keeping the commemorative pencils. I've rounded up those, along with the specialty pens, from junk drawers and throughout the house. They all now mingle inside a ceramic pencil holder formerly kept on my work desk. Imprinted on its side is this unattributed quote: "Organized people are just too lazy to look for things." Guess that explains the missing scissors.

What's in that canister is in many ways the story, or maybe I should say stories, of our lives. Do you realize how many important people, places, and things that have meaning to you and your family are represented on writing utensils? Go ahead, look through your office and junk drawers to find out. At our house, in no particular order, you'll find the following.

There are two green pencils that the kids received for perfect attendance in elementary school. The two fanciest pencils in our stash are gold-hued with black erasers and came from Hotel Edison in Midtown Manhattan, steps away from Times Square from a family trip to New York City. That special trip took place the fall of our fortieth wedding anniversary.

We have six news-oriented pencils—two red No. 2s touting, "Your best in local news," from *The Star Tribune* in Attica, Indiana, my 1980s employer (now called *The Fountain County Neighbor*), and three from *The Courier-Times* where I worked for thirty-one years in New Castle, Indiana. These are Trojan green, the city's school color, and two of the pencils proclaim, "#1 in local news."

Another pencil, from the one-time Newseum in Washington, D.C., declares, "News Junkie," on its side. "Indiana Bicentennial 1816-2016," is one-of-a-kind in a collection of few-of-a-kinds.

THE PENS, THOUGH, TAKE a bit longer to describe than do the pencils. My favorite is more prize than pen, the ink now bone-dry. It reads: "School Spelling Champion 1967 *The Hammond Times*." It is Brian's participation keepsake for competing in the citywide competition after winning his own Edison Junior High School championship. He nailed the word RESTAURANT at his school, only to falter on PARASOL at the city level.

Ben routinely refers to his father as a wordsmith, even though *I'm* supposed to be the writer in the house.

Also no longer with ink is Brian's childhood pen, proclaiming the name of his favorite baseball team, the Chicago White Sox.

Two spent ink pens display the Standard Oil logo. One is from an insurance agent, the other from Brian's late father's employer, recognizing a work-safety designation.

There are pens from vacations, such as a hotel freebie from a Florida resort, and clever gift-shop novelties including a spinning planet Earth at the top of two Smithsonian pens. There's a wonderful wooden-gavel pen from the U.S. Capitol.

I have a pen that served as a Congressional-luncheon favor from an event I covered on Capitol Hill while representing my newspaper group.

Then there are pens that came to us in still more varieties of ways. My author friend, Sandy Moore, gives away pens that promote her novels, and an acquaintance promotes the German shepherds he raises.

There are commemorative pens from as eclectic places as the one-time Lincoln Museum in Fort Wayne, Indiana, and the Louisville Slugger gift shop in Kentucky. My grade-five teacher, Mrs. Sipahigil, gifted me with a pen, "Baskets by Jeanne," stamped on it. She's quite the basketmaker.

Others commemorate Henry County Indiana Extension Homemakers, an organization that made me an honorary member, and Henry County Academy for Community Leadership, a local course I completed. There's a work pen from a woman I interviewed who loaned it to me when mine went dry. When I offered to return it upon discovering that I accidentally made off with it, she laughed and said to keep it. It's a fine pen. I should put it into regular service.

Each writing utensil has a memory—of people we've recently met or of those we've known well, of special events, places, or organizations along life's path. We never started out determined to collect pens or pencils, but a good number seemed to collect us.

IRONICALLY, THE MOST EXPENSIVE, yet least-cared-about pens in our collection are the classy, heavy-grade, silver-or-gold-toned numbers that came to us on special occasions. I bet you have a few: from graduation gifts and work anniversaries or maybe from occasions when folks simply didn't know what else to buy. No longer isolated inside their boxes, the pens now stand tall and keep company with the others.

Does anyone actually use the fancy ones? To my hand, they are too weighty, causing the words to slog along rather than glide across a page. I need to write with speed, or think I do, a remnant of my newspaper-interviewing days.

These pricey pens are the figureheads of the writing world, more appropriate in ceremonial situations or reclining comfortably in a drawer, than doing the blue-collar grunt work of the gel pen that rolls around at the bottom of my purse.

Writing utensils make for a great collection. They are inexpensive, often free, plentiful, useful, can be distinctive, and take up little space. Sometimes, they seem to hide. Still, they're not as shy as scissors.

If you're looking to start an entertaining, yet inexpensive collection for your kids, grandkids, or for yourself, these simple tools are write on.

I won't say pardon the pun because I'm not sorry.

16

Jamming with the shredder

AS A YOUNG GIRL, I overheard a comment that never left me: "If only I had saved that one piece of paper..."

I felt sad that the person's important paper came up missing, vowing silently that when I grew up, I'd make sure to save *all the papers*. At least all the papers that I perceived as important to our family. I have tried to do just that. Over time, those added up to a lot of trees reduced to paper form that were stored and stacked into attic totes.

Along the way, it had become my habit to retain the financial statements, check registries, tax returns, and receipts, instead of deciding what needed to go. You know the cliché: Better safe than sorry.

My method became loading a year's worth of records into whatever storage materials we had on hand during a moment of organization: manila envelopes, office files, and clear, storage sleeves. Then I added those to the layers of previous years' paperwork inside a larger container. Once one tub filled, I started another.

I PUT DECISIONS ABOUT what papers to eliminate from our financial lives on hold until after I got through the softer side of attic memory lane: Ben's baseball uniforms and trophies, Sam's Scouting keepsakes, my tap shoes, and all the rest.

Finally, in the season of cleaning out, the goal came down to editing paperwork to its essence, keeping only relevant pieces. I won't offer advice on how to do that, lest you come up short on "that one piece of paper" that perhaps you truly need.

What a hassle it is to misplace important papers such as a mortgage deed or vehicle title. Of course, there are means to replace them, but it takes more time and effort than any of us want to deal with. Trust me on this. We once had to replace a vehicle title. And when do we need a vehicle title? Quickly; when we are selling a vehicle. So yeah.

Even with my mountain range of paper, I always try to single out those key items and a few others besides, and lock them away in a secure safe-deposit box off site.

That said, there are limits to what we need to save. In an ideal world, many pieces of paper can be destroyed once official statements are verified.

Surely it's safe that a collection of defunct bank-account information from a community we haven't lived nor banked in since the 1980s can be shredded. Same goes for a whole lot more, including a childhood savings account registry from a bank that no longer exists by that name.

MY MAIN PROBLEM WITH old paperwork had become more to do with not having eliminated much of it over the decades. Therefore, insurance and financial policies, account numbers, and that golden ticket to fraud, Social Security numbers, remained intact on a variety of statements. I am astounded to see how decades ago, the SS number appeared on everything. Even college-class receipts contained that number right there at the top.

Receipts are tucked deeply into textbooks and possibly remain there when the books return to the college bookstore, or maybe papers fall to the floor without our realizing it, for anyone's eyes to see. I recently found one such receipt inside an old college notebook of Brian's.

Back then, we didn't treat the privacy of those numbers as anything that mattered so much. Now we know to guard Social Security and credit-card numbers with our lives!

Drivers' license numbers in some places may still possibly be the same as Social Security numbers. That's no longer the case in my state. Yet, some people may be too casual in using or revealing those numbers. We might dictate them aloud in a public space if a clerk needed them in order to take advantage of a quick discount.

Now Americans hire security companies to scan the universe to make sure some anonymous crook isn't using our numbers and stealing our data for evil purposes. Yet it still happens. Within eleven recent months, our credit card got hacked once successfully, and another time unsuccessfully. Each incident, however, resulted in closing the account and getting a new one.

I HAD WANTED A SHREDDER for a long time but once the cleaning-out process began, we *needed* one. I know there are professional services for shredding, but I want to *witness* everything being destroyed. It doesn't work for me to drop it all off for others to shred while I wonder who has access to the gold in them-there hills of paper. I need to either see the paper trail turn into tiny bits of paper, or do it myself.

So, I did it myself when Brian bought a shredder.

I almost broke it the first time out.

I had never used one of these machines in my life. If you haven't either, how it works is to run sheets of paper through a thin, horizontal opening where blades slice the paper into small, skinny strips. The strips fall into a wastebasket-type container. To destroy all financial information for one random year, for example, takes about an hour in one setting. This project would take a while.

While working away on the task at hand, I gave some thought to what we could do with stacks of paper shreds that were accumulating. I decided they would make cushiony beds for storing Christmas ornaments and for packing up Grandma's antique cups and saucers. They could also make themselves useful by serving as fine filler in gift bags for years to come.

I found the shredding process so satisfying, the whirl of the blades so efficient, that I went to town with the papers. I found myself in the zone! Then I became too confident and overplayed my hand.

The machine jammed.

I wanted to solve the problem but wouldn't you know, about that time, as though he possesses some kind of superpower to sense a problem (I think it's the retired principal in him), Brian called cheerfully up the stairs that leads to our study. "How's it going with the shredding?" he asked.

Silence.

Confession.

"I jammed it."

That's not what he wanted to hear.

After Brian looked at it and expressed his disappointment about my ruining the shredder on its debut outing, I got out the instruction manual and followed the directions for dislodging a jam. It worked! Crisis averted!

Another day, however, every time I ran the shredder, Brian's TV downstairs started going haywire.

"How do you know it's the shredder causing it?" I asked Brian.

"I looked online and it says so," he answered.

Nice. *Not.* So, I'd move this task to non-TV-watching hours. Would this job ever get finished?

Brian said we should simply burn the paperwork. Great idea, other than we don't have a fireplace, firepit, nor any worthy method of fiery destruction.

I improvised; not something one should probably try when dealing with fire. I took a galvanized tub, added torn-and-crumpled pieces of the paper, and set it ablaze. It kind of scared me, as the sparks and blackened paper rose, even on a non-breezy day.

I drenched the mess with a bucket of water, only to discover that due to the heat from the tub, we then had a blackened circle on our lawn. I wonder if they can see it from space.

A friend with a firepit took pity on me, offering to burn some documents in a more efficient manner. I took her up on the offer, arriving with a few years' worth of paperwork.

It took longer than anticipated, and as much as I appreciate her kindness, after that evening, it didn't seem fair to take any more hours out of her life for the express purpose of watching our papers roast.

I know. It seems like a ridiculous problem, but I had saved a ridiculous amount of paper. It took forty-two years to create the mountain, and would require some time to tear it down.

WHILE SORTING ALL THIS paperwork, I glanced at some ways we spent money over those years, as detailed in the canceled checks, registries, and bank statements. There were the normal utility bills, of course; the church and other charitable donations, groceries, clothes, mortgage, taxes, insurances, and stuff for the house.

There were the lifestyle choices such as baseball lessons for Ben, vacations, and all the things one spends money on through the years. But I didn't get lost in those handwritten checks, nor travel too deeply into the memories involved. Money used wisely; money squandered—the story of humanity.

Shredding arrived in our household as an overdue method of

putting all that behind us so we could move forward. Now we have a fresh start with new decisions to implement about going even more paperless whenever that option is available and makes sense.

It wasn't hard to decide to toss defunct bank records of ancestors whose paperwork I somehow inherited, their Social Security numbers long since retired, their estates settled, or to shred my parents' check registries that included a notation inside one for payment of our wedding cake.

I've reached the end of this personal-paper purge. But that doesn't mean it's the end of paperwork. We'll be using that shredder regularly from now on.

I'll try hard not to get us in a jam.

Or, to become visible from space.

17

Screen cleaning

IN THE SAME WAY that we aren't privy to the clutter inside the minds of others, or ushered up to their attics or down to their basements to see what's all in storage, so it goes with one another's various computer-and-cellphone screens and devices.

If I know you're coming to my house, I'll put everything else I'm doing aside to straighten the family room and give the guest-bathroom facilities a good swish with the cleanser and brush.

But neither friends nor the public can see the notices to update this or that on my cellphone, which I tend to ignore, or the zillion old emails that I forget to delete off the laptop, or, in reality, think I might need again.

It's the same old story as that of the physical attic above us. There might be something there I hang onto, rather than regret one day that I had let it go. Then before you know it, forty years pass and the containers are stacked high. Or, there are 8,701 emails, most of which should have been deleted on day one of their arrival.

I still think of the laptop used for the writing of this book as being new. It's not. By the time you are reading the book, the computer will be a few years old. In people years, it's a preschooler but in computer years, it's an aging adult with wrinkles.

I still have an old-time mindset that it takes a hundred years, fifty at the least, for an object to be old or antique. The personal-computer age changed all that.

Those who regularly get new phones, computers, and related devices may scoff at my old-school outlook, but there it is, and I'm not alone.

Still, whatever your approach is to old files, photos, emails, and other virtual information that stick around your online world, there are things we should be doing to maintain the health and safety of our computers, as well as our own sanity.

Having retired from my newspaper career, I went through and deleted from my phone photos from most of the stories I've written (saving back a few particularly sentimental ones for posterity). Same with the photos I uploaded, downloaded, formatted, and captioned from others while working from home during the pandemic.

I'm also going through old personal files and photos that I've kept tucked here and there inside computer folders, or dragged-and-dropped out of the way. These things are clutter, no different from the totes full of physical clothing and papers eliminated from attic storage.

I also deleted an app or several that I no longer want; filled, and emptied the desktop trash can many times.

HAVE YOU EVER HAD this happen? New to my first social media outlet several years ago, I became so enamored with reconnecting to old friends, family members, current and former co-workers, I started reaching out to everyone I had ever remotely known or remembered and to whomever the particular social media outlet suggested I might wish to contact.

"Hi, it's me! Do you remember attending my birthday party when we were in first grade? I have a picture of you somewhere. I'll try to find it and send you a copy if you would like!"

No response came from that long-lost classmate after I opened with all that. (I can see why now. That was Over. The. Top.)

I nearly cried from delight when our sons instantly accepted me into their online networks.

Then one day I reached out to someone I hadn't seen in years. I waited. No response. Maybe the person didn't see my howdy-do, I thought, so I sent another.

After that, I found that the person's online profile had "disappeared." *How slow to catch on could I be?* I wondered, feeling more than a bit humiliated as it finally clicked. Yep, I'd apparently been blocked. And I'm not talking about the finishing technique on a hand-knitted sweater.

At that moment, I realized that it's not necessary nor advisable to have online friendships with *everyone* I have ever known.

ALONG WITH MAKING SURE that our devices contain the proper filters, cybersecurity programs, and the clutter is cleaned out, there's another issue we sometimes face.

What do we do about the contact information and social media contacts of people who have, ahem, passed away? Am I the only one who finds it a tad disturbing when a deceased person's photo suddenly pops up with a reminder that it's their birthday? I asked that very question once on social media and got a surprise in that some folks like that reminder, and continue to post something on the person's page. It serves as a modern-day memorial.

And what do we want to do about our own platforms and passwords when we're unable to maintain them? Do we have a plan for our online profiles to disappear when we do? Have you shared your passcodes and other login information with someone trustworthy who will handle that? Have you considered putting such things inside your important-paper files? Maybe with your will? And do you have people in your life who will be able to get to these computer-related keys to your kingdom in case something should happen to you?

These are concerns easy to keep high on shelves out of the way, or tucked into the corners of the to-do lists inside our minds that never quite make it into action plans.

They are the attics and basements of our online and cellphone lives. What do you keep in yours?

WHILE MANY OR EVEN most people don't maintain a literal paper trail of their lives in plastic containers that require heavy lifting, there is a world of financial information stored behind our screens.

There are many aspects of our online lives and the footprints we leave. I predict these issues will become even more complex as the years pass.

While you no longer hear so much about people beating rugs and washing walls as part of their spring-cleaning rituals, perhaps it's time to set aside some regular time for screen cleaning.

18

The last address book?

I BOUGHT THE BIG, blue address book twenty years into our marriage. We were in the heart of raising our sons. We were middle age—already! Funny, but now I think of that time period as part of our younger years.

The book replaced a small, brown one that had seen better days, mainly because people in our orbit had moved multiple times advancing their careers or upgrading their addresses. Often, their old information had been scribbled out, and new pages containing their new digs and phone numbers were added.

When I finished transferring people's information to the clean, new pages, I remember thinking: *This will be the last address book we'll ever own.*

Another twenty years passed and I'm proven wrong. The blue book had gotten quite a workout in those years: two decades spent looking up addresses for Christmas cards and other special occasions, and mostly, for adding updates as people's lives continue to evolve.

It held together with clear postal tape, and now, it seems that so many of the people listed, such as elderly relatives, have passed away. Or they had retired or moved on from the professional relationships we had with them such as a doctor, dentist, baseball coaches, or Scout leaders.

They had been with us for seasons of life that were behind us now; our connections possibly intense or simply pleasant for a time, but long term, were not sustainable.

And what possible reason would I need to keep contact information for the high school girlfriend of a son's best friend? Especially since my son is closer to middle age than to his teens. Why did I even have her number to begin with?

These days we need updates inside address books in addition to mere addresses. We need cellphone numbers. There's no master phone book to go to for those. When folks decide to drop the landline, those who care about them from a distance, can suddenly have no way to reach them quickly. It's something to think about with your older loved ones in order to stay current with their contact information.

I like paper backup, and while that may seem old-fashioned, I've been called upon for such information, and I'm glad I have it. I could do better on keeping it updated, though.

I MADE A TRIP to a local office-supply store to select a new, paper address book. The aisle with the year's crop of annual-planner calendars burst with products in an assortment of styles and sizes. There were floral versions as well as expensive-looking, leather ones that seemed suitable for important executives.

Many calendars offer much more than dates; they include such specialty-themed upgrades as daily scriptures, gardening tips, or motivational thoughts. There are calendars with the emphasis on either a day, week, or month, and calendars with large blocks of blank daily space—ideal for using at a work desk.

There are even calendars where you write in the dates for each month and pen in the correct year, a "universal" calendar.

But what there are not on that aisle are address books.

I walked around, taking in the office-and-school supplies, but not finding what I needed.

Maybe I'm too late by a few years. Does anyone *but* me keep an address book up to date in the same way that our folks before us did?

Our parents maintained these address records, keeping them updated. These objects are treasure troves of contact information for friends and family that date back many decades. The address books are in rough shape, though, because our parents stopped short of replacing old ones with new.

But that's their charm. They are time capsules of people and their places of residences and relationships. And it's all written in our mothers' hands. It's lovely and personal and a little sad to see their handwriting again. Their distinctive penmanship tugs at my heart.

When purging so many papers and objects, it's easy to become discouraged with the overflow that remains. I considered pitching those old address books that feature the casts of characters that made up our families' lives through the years.

Brian confirmed that we should keep them and I'm happy for the persuasion.

BACK TO THE STORE. I found some address books. A small selection, those in stock weren't showcased prominently, resting on a bottom shelf.

I possibly had the distinction of being the only human on the planet visiting a brick-and-mortar store that day expressly in search of a new, paper address book.

I selected a bright-red version. It doesn't say ADDRESSES on the front as the old blue one does, but I'll know, and it will be easy to locate inside the office-supply cabinet.

When I got it home I opened it up alongside the old one. I thought I'd start the process of transferring the names, printing by hand each one along with the related information.

But then, after a short while, I felt a wave of apprehension, and closed them both. I would have to make decisions about who to keep and who to omit from the contacts. Why is this a tough call?

I always liked the now-retired woman who completed our income taxes for many years. I disliked leaving her out, even though I doubted that I'd be calling her simply for a pleasant visit.

We no longer get our carpet professionally cleaned since we bought our own shampooer. I suppose I could let the professional carpet cleaner's contact information slide. But on second thought, what if we make a horrible mess and need some special expertise? Better save it.

I spot the address of a couple who were fine neighbors at a previous location. The husband passed away probably fifteen years ago, but I haven't stopped at their home in twenty years, even though she lives only a few miles away. Do I save her address? Does she even live there now? I feel a stab of guilt for not taking half an hour out of twenty years to pull into her driveway and shoot the breeze with this sweet woman.

WHAT'S SAD IS TO see all the addresses that no longer hold loved ones behind their front doors. Aunts and uncles, now gone. Divorces. People who were part of our lives for a limited reason or season. People who were once major players on the teams, sports or otherwise, in our lives.

Then I spot the address of my kindergarten teacher, Miss Grace Kalter, whom without fail sends a Christmas card each year. She even came to not one but two of my book signings in my hometown library.

And there are newer addresses: those for the places our kids now call home, those for work friends who have moved away or retired but who are not forgotten.

This address-book stuff takes a generous supply of emotional energy to update in the new, red book, as well as a task that requires a chunk of time to sit down and finish.

I haven't found myself in the right frame of mind yet to get the red book fully in order. It's a project; one that will take some time to work through.

But I do believe it will be our last address book.

At least there are plenty of extra pages. I hope we'll need them. In my book, people are a good thing to both keep and add to one's life—and to one's address book.

19

What's in your bag?

A FEW YEARS AGO, I wrote a speech for some women's programs with the title, "What's on your bucket list?" The presentation includes a group-participation exercise where attendees are invited to share what's on their lists.

Common dreams include potential trips to Hawaii and Europe with an occasional Holy Land mentioned as a crowd favorite. In my non-scientific survey, Hawaii leads the pack as tops on women's bucket lists for desired travel destinations.

One dream expressed, however, stands out from the rest because it's so unique. The dreamer offers a different take from the fantasy-trips-of-a-lifetime goals often expressed. She said that her goal is to leave this world with no more physical belongings than what will fit into a single bag.

Her idea is that we can't take the things of this world with us into eternity, so our emphasis shouldn't be on stuff.

I don't think I'll ever forget her comments.

While I have given much thought to her answer, I still can't come up with a concise list of what I'd like inside my bag as final belongings. I imagine negotiating for a bigger bag. That only means I'm far too rooted in this world. I'll give it a shot, though.

I would start with family photos that predate cellphone pictures. We have numerous photo albums lining our bookshelves, and in addition to those, piles and files more that have not been placed into albums.

It's clear that not even a fraction of those photos would fit into one reasonably sized bag. How could I possibly pare down the photos to essential keepers?

Some of you are possibly thinking there's a simple solution. Remedies might involve placing these photos on discs, thumb drives, in clouds or inside advanced means of cool-kid technology. Problem is that technology evolves and its permanent-storage aspects are not sustainable. (VCR, anyone?)

That's why I want to stick with photos that can be held in one's hand and viewed easily when, say I'm in a nursing home, and want to review a lifetime of special memories.

I wouldn't forget my highlighted Bible and notes from various Bible studies. Here's a question. Could I carry a purse in addition to the bag? Okay, this is a hypothetical exercise, so there's no one to ask. Let's say no, because that is clearly the intent of the lady's point. And I know: to ask the question is missing that point. But it's also demonstrating where I'm coming from regarding this concept. You can see that I have a way to go regarding this topic.

OFTEN DURING THIS PROCESS of cleaning out the attic, I've wondered what I would pack for the long-term care home should I go live there. I think of those things mentioned above, but add to them the large crate holding a lifetime of cards and letters from closest friends and family members.

Friend Gay gets the prize for the largest number of handwritten letters and notes that keep coming, even in the digital age, more than forty years into our friendship. I would want those, as well as my mother's letters. I would like to keep the beautiful handmade cards I've saved, such as those from Debbie, Marilyn, Cheryl, and Donna. Friend Suzy recently asked if I still have her homemade poinsettia-themed Christmas card.

I'd need my laptop (or whatever similar technology in use then). It contains years of emails and contact information, and besides, I could keep generating email.

Will there even *be* email then? I hear that it's already outdated for many people. I happen to love it immeasurably more than text messaging. With it my fingers fly over a spacious keyboard, making not music but words, thanks to Ethel Sharp teaching me how to type. Let's just say there's a reason that my fingers are the one area of my body that have never had a weight issue.

Communication is my love language. How will we stay in touch in the years to come?

If I must go into long-term care or into a small apartment, I also would want a big purse and a large tote bag along with a cosmetics bag full of my favorite products; a twenty-times magnification mirror, and maybe some jewelry. I would like for the wall next to my bed installed with bookcases to hold a lifetime of photo albums and memorabilia.

Could be by then I won't need all those photos (including the vintage ones) as they may all be floating in a cloud somewhere and be available for viewing on any device or whatever they are calling such things then. Just make sure someone pays my cloud-storage bill.

But who am I kidding? It would be time to truly pare down. I can't see anyone installing those bookshelves or filling them with old photo albums. No one will rent me a cloud. But would someone please promise to keep me stocked in lipstick and eyeliner?

SOMETHING I'VE NOTICED IN my own life and in the lives of others, is that the older we get, the fewer *things* we need or want. We spend the first half century of our lives "getting," then whatever time remains of the second half, "getting rid" of.

Friend Patti once asked (well, more than once) if she can have my Sellers cabinet when I'm gone. I told her yes, but the fact that she's merely a few years my junior makes me smile. I picture myself in my long-term care home watching Patti push my wheeled baking cabinet through the hallways. I imagine following her to see where she'll put it, but there's nowhere to be found. That's the point. Sometimes when we finally get around to the getting of something we always wanted, we no longer want nor need it.

Maybe I should have a goal of no bags whatsoever. None of us will take even one to the grave. Our hands will be empty, but God willing, our hearts will be full.

20

*Postcards and property;
dishes and diamonds*

NO MATTER IF YOU'RE from a place on the map that many describe as, "somewhere," or from a community that others label, "nowhere," your life comes with interesting, even historic twists and turns. Truth is, *every* place is "somewhere." It's your home.

Everyone's life has a story. You need only to *see* it.

Have you ever thought about what your ancestors experienced? I think of this when I run across photos or belongings from those who came before me.

In particular, I'm thinking about two women—"ansisters," if you will—who are from the same tiny Indiana community where Dad and his people lived, a handful of miles from our farm. One is my great-grandmother, Sarah, nicknamed "Sally Ann;" the other, Grace, a distant aunt.

Sally Ann had two brushes with what we today refer to as American history. She passed down these oral-history stories to her daughter, who would tell them to her only granddaughter—me.

Both memories are simple, with few details, but they are rich in what they do to my imagination.

ONE TALE HAPPENED TO Sally Ann as a girl in her family's garden. The story goes that a Native American came around and stood there, leaving after given a cucumber. While this took place pre-Civil War, I heard about it as a child and years later, ran it by an Indiana-history college professor. He asked questions about the place and time, then concluded that yes, indeed, it is possible that this happened. Were they neighbors? Was this a unique visit? We'll probably never know.

Sally Ann also shared how she got up in the night in April 1865 to travel a dozen or so miles north to see the Lincoln Funeral Train, which headed west through the region. The train carried the body of slain President Abraham Lincoln on his final earthly journey to his resting place in the state capital of Springfield, Illinois.

How I'd love to roll the tape of her experience; to witness what she saw regarding these moments in national history. As the Union paused in deep mourning, Sally Ann paid her respects in person, due to her place near the train route.

Some belongings in my home were hers first, such as a set of white dishes. Grandma inherited the china, which is adorned with large, gold-hued leaves, stored behind wooden doors inside a buffet. Then Mom kept the dish set in the same place, never once using it that I recall. I think she feared those dishes might break. Because they remained out of sight, except when I opened the wooden doors for a peek, I viewed them with high regard, afraid to touch them.

The story goes that someone once offered a thousand dollars for the circa-1900 set. It seems an incredibly lofty price. Of course, times and tastes change, and if placed on even a thrift-shop shelf today, the dishes might go ignored.

I rarely use the heirloom dishes, which research shows

originated from WACO China of East Liverpool, Ohio. Today, they rest behind clear glass in our dining room, for all to see, rather than behind wooden doors where they previously remained unseen. Recently, I decided to get some of the matching serving pieces out and showcase them in our kitchen. Their value to me is that the full set has remained in the family for about 125 years.

GRACE'S LIFE OVERLAPS SALLY Ann's but she lived about three decades longer. The youngest of her siblings, she passed away in the middle 1960s, the last of her generation in my extended family on that side.

I have a vague memory of looking up from my crib to see her, and at about age four, going with my parents to visit the widowed Grace when she lived inside a long-term care home. My folks took her my mother's signature spice cake as a treat.

Most of what I know about Grace is from the backs of numerous colorful postcards she wrote on and mailed to her family in the first decade of the 1900s. She had left our little county for the state capital of Indianapolis. The cards are intriguing as they feature city scenes from so long ago that remain relevant today such as the 1888 Soldiers and Sailors Monument well known on Monument Circle.

Another Indianapolis monument is featured on a postcard depicting University Park. I looked with a magnifying glass at tiny type on the featured monument. It is the name Schuyler Colfax, who served as Ulysses S. Grant's vice president. The statue remains today but the setting looks entirely different with the modern cityscape surrounding it.

Another postcard from 1911 is Military Park, the oldest park in Indianapolis, built in 1852.

Two postcards are of Union Station, also identified as Union Passenger Station. It is noted as the oldest union station in the world. Who knew?

Grace is fond of drama on her cards, remarking about the weather, how she's feeling, who in the family had written to her—or not, and when she will be home for a visit.

One reads, "I suppose Donnie (her sister, Dad's grandmother) told you I have no news." Another states, "I am so hot tonight that I am nearly dead." Yet another card reads, "Sunday and I am nearly froze."

I read them with expectation, waiting these many decades later, for Grace to inform us about national happenings of her day. I want to learn about more important news than the weather.

Yet I realize that I am the same, preferring to dive into my own, personal storyline when writing to or speaking with a friend over exploring extraordinary national or world history in the making.

I think that as history unfolds, there are periods when it doesn't feel particularly historic, but rather, simply life as usual. Plus, at the time, we are catching up with friends and family, absorbed in our own storylines, and not thinking that anyone will years later read what we share.

Grace married, but didn't have children. Along with her postcards, I also inherited a pendant that Mom said Grace's husband brought back from France when he served in World War I. Grace handed it down to Dad, and eventually it came to me.

The pendant is on a necklace that I wear on rare occasions. It is a dangly piece, fully intact. Its charm is in its family history over any dollar value.

I FEEL VAGUELY SAD that Grace never had any closer-to-her living descendants in which to will her belongings than to my father. Maybe Dad helped her through the years in ways I couldn't have realized as a young child. Maybe she felt closer to him than to anyone still living. That's apparently the case.

Grace is noted for leaving Dad her Packard, a car my folks kept

THERE'S A CLYDESDALE IN THE ATTIC

and drove as the family vehicle; a beautiful platinum-gold ring with a trio of diamonds, and, a place in Florida.

I remember the car, which Dad always praised, but it's the ring and the Florida property that stayed around longer. Curiously, by today's standards, my folks never visited Florida with the purpose of checking out that real estate inheritance.

While it remained a topic mentioned occasionally, at some point the property sold from a distance. As I got older, I had to wonder if they received a reasonable price. I know that whatever their profit, I didn't see any lifestyle changes on our farm, nor any new Packards in the driveway. Yet I'm sure whatever money came in was turned back into the farm.

Grace's gracious bequests were most appreciated but my folks didn't become wealthy from them. The profit may have been tidy or quite small—I don't know. I couldn't even say where the property had been located.

At least I couldn't until I started writing this book. Guess I only needed to check under the bed.

Tim often gifted me with containers of family heirlooms. I didn't know, nor think, that Grace's papers still existed. At the time that Tim passed a box of her memorabilia to me, I slid it under a guest-room bed and forgot about it.

One day I looked under the bed in search of a flat box of wreaths when the container of Grace's papers got in the way. I lifted it out and rifled through the dense stack of documents, still overwhelmed with the idea of sorting through these old papers that had no real value. Yet these papers were possibly rich in family history—if only I had the time and drive to connect the dots.

Mixed in with the paperwork were a few unexpected photos. Then, I spotted her: an older woman, in front of a small cottage. Behind her were more houses that looked similar to hers. I flipped over the pictures to learn the identity: Grace!

Suddenly, I knew. *This* had to be the property in Florida that

Grace owned and left to my folks. Then I found letters to Dad that spoke of her Orlando bank. These offered instructions about where to locate her final written wishes and important papers (probably the very ones I went through at that moment).

The photos appear as from the 1950s. Grace lived another decade, ending up back in Indiana near my parents. Her "mind wasn't good," as my parents described, regarding her final years. Perhaps she had what would now be described as dementia or Alzheimer's disease.

The diamond ring stayed in the family another forty years after Grace's passing. My parents tucked it inside a safe.

As a little girl, I enjoyed reaching into the safe and examining a few old coins and this ring. Sometimes I slipped it onto my middle or index finger and wore the too-big diamond ring around the house briefly, feeling as extravagant as Mrs. Howell on *Gilligan's Island*. I admired the three sparkling stones mounted flat inside the vintage setting, a striking, unusual design in the 1960s-'70s.

The ring felt too fancy for modern wear, and eventually sold on consignment in a jewelry store. Proceeds weren't life changing for anyone, but went to help pay Mom's bills that month.

I wish I had bought the heirloom for the appraised amount and kept it. I've never seen a ring such as it, but could see myself wearing and it enjoying it the rest of my life, or, separating the diamonds into earrings and a pendant. At the time, though, our family had more pressing expenses than a fancy old ring.

I THINK OF ALL the interesting topics these two women represent: one had contact with a Native American in early-Indiana history; then saw the actual Lincoln Funeral Train in 1865. The other left home to become a working woman in her state's capital in the early 1900s; marrying a World War I veteran; owning a Packard, property in Florida, and a remarkable ring.

I wonder what more they could share about life, and the history they lived, the challenges, and joys they experienced. One departed this earth many years before I arrived; the other's life intersected mine for a few years in a marginal way.

Yet I think of them today. *Ansisters.*

As with them, I have had moments that some might one day find historic: covering the 2017 presidential inauguration and Women's March for a newspaper group; photographing such public figures as basketball great Larry Bird and President Ronald Reagan; interacting and speaking briefly with Vice President Mike Pence of Indiana, and covering a speech by another Hoosier, former Vice President Dan Quayle.

I briefly shook hands with Muhammad Ali; photographed and wrote about my childhood pop-music crush, David Cassidy; spent time with noted author Joyce Maynard; and had audience as a reporter with former Indiana Gov. Robert Orr inside his Statehouse office. I remember the assassination of President John F. Kennedy, and the 9/11 horror.

Most of all, I will always treasure the trip of a lifetime to Israel. It felt at once like being dropped into both the Old and New Testaments. The Bible went from black and white to living color, where it remains.

I'll keep the photo of Grace posed in front of her Florida cottage, along with letters she sent Dad, and the vintage postcards. The rest won't return to under the bed; the wreaths will have the space to themselves.

The two women never described themselves as writers, yet their stories survive. What about you? Are you telling your stories? Are you recording the details for future generations to learn from, admire, or simply wonder about?

Packards and property, dishes and diamonds may come and go, but stories are priceless and can be both kept and shared. Sometimes in that process, we touch history—because it touches us first.

21

Getting carried away

FOR THE LAST FORTY-FIVE years, a little piece of caramel-colored luggage, likely from the 1950s, has been without work. In all that time, it sat empty inside our basement, outbuilding, or attic, inside or outside the various properties we called and call home.

So why keep it around?

Often we keep objects because of what they might mean to us in the future. This one stayed because of what it meant in the past. Every time I saw it, it reminded me of good times spent during all the years of my youth.

During those childhood-and-teen years, the travel case is where I packed a nightie, toothbrush, hair brush, and later makeup, along with a simple change of clothes for the next day. The overnighter went with me to homes of friends or relatives. I miss the days of such simplicity in packing. Each trip meant plans that we had for fun, or if not, I knew we would make new ones as we went along.

117

You can tell that the little carrier is actually the cosmetics' case that came as part of a luggage set. My folks owned a couple coordinating suitcases, making up a three-piece ensemble. I have no idea where that luggage is now. I don't even know if my parents purchased the set or if it was handed down in the family. Relatives may have bought the set for, say, trips to Florida, or to some other interesting destination I'll never know about.

The suitcases might be much older than I imagine. They could be inherited from Dad's Great-Aunt Grace, whom you met in a previous chapter.

I've always been one who liked to *go*, to have plans! (Still do, as a matter of fact.) I can't count the Friday-night sleepovers at my friend Cheryl's house, to my older-brother David's family's home, or to visit an assortment of other girlfriends through the years.

Everywhere I went in those golden days of youth, if the trip included spending the night, the travel case went along. Tells you something about traveling light—one thing you'll never catch me doing now.

Even if Brian and I are heading out for a few hours to visit our kids or friends, before we hit the road, he's waiting for me with the car running as I round up a stack of paperwork, a book I'm reading, a lesson I'm working on, or a magazine I'm flipping through, complete with a travel mug full of ice water. (If we're going far, maybe I'll have all those things.)

The travel case once harbored a distinctive scent, probably that of long-ago mothballs. Mom tended to liberally apply those to everything stowed away at our house. But to me, oddly, the particular smell combined with this travel case translated into the scent of fun.

It no longer carries any scent at all; only memories. And that's why it's time to say goodbye.

Now don't go and make this harder on me by suggesting what I *could* use it for, or store inside, or how I could spruce it up, or learn to travel light again.

If I had larger, vintage suitcases to match, I would probably take the suggestion that Tim once made. He said old suitcases make great storage containers for old papers and photos. Yes, the three-piece set could provide a smart look, stacked together and filled with family photos or papers. Wish I had them, but not enough to go on a search to collect look-alikes for the little case.

THERE ARE OTHER SUITCASES and duffel bags that you and I may want to keep because they are of current style and function. At my house, we've filled the larger ones with the smaller ones and now stow them together in a guest-bedroom closet. Our favorites for travel are properly tagged and ready to go whenever we get the chance.

A name and cell number found on the outside of one particular suitcase apparently served its purpose beautifully when we took our first family trip to New York City—and our first activity in The Big Apple involved picking up and carrying off someone else's suitcase that looked exactly like ours.

Right before the trip, we had ironically joked about how unlikely *that* scenario would be, given Brian's somewhat unique suitcase size and color.

The airport contacted us before we even noticed the error, due I imagine, to the tag dangling from our actual luggage that the other passenger turned in. Our driver got us back to the airport, the mix-up remedied in short order. At least the luggage tag served as back up for the airline one. So much for thinking of Brian's large, teal suitcase as among the few of a kind.

As for my childhood-travel companion, I said farewell. I no longer need to save everything that comes with a story, nor that reminds me of still another story. I've reached a tipping point where there's often more joy in the getting rid of a thing than in the saving

119

of it (and stacking, and putting away, and caring for, or not caring for).

I carried it away one last time, to a favorite donation site, and wished it happy travels on its next assignment.

22

One woman's trash

WHILE MANY OF US try to donate things we no longer want that remain useful, there are more options to consider than we might realize.

Donating used-but-still-useful items can be anonymous actions regarding a recipient, yet at the same time, one where you get charitable receipts for tax purposes. Or, it can be a hands-on, personalized activity where you may or may not get a deduction, yet provide a wonderful service.

We can also let it be known we have belongings that are up for grabs and spread the net wide for those who might want them. We can even personally pinpoint people whom we think might have special interests. We can bless folks in the process. And who gets blessed while blessing others? Try it and see!

We had a piece of heavy, awkward exercise equipment we wanted gone. But instead of wrestling it down a flight of stairs and figuring out how to get it off the property, I reached out on social media to see if anyone wanted it. Stipulations were posted up front to fend off any hard feelings when someone couldn't meet requirements such as a pickup deadline—or a firm commitment. (Someone saying, "I *might* want it," doesn't get the piece out of my house and can leave a cleaning-out project on deep hold.)

I stated that the freebie had to be removed by a certain date and that the new owner needed to arrive accompanied by a strong back so the two of them could move it downstairs.

To my delight, a younger-generation family member wanted it, came and got it with a good helper, and there's our happy ending to that story.

WE HANG FERNS ON our back porch each spring where they thrive through hot Midwestern summers. Right before the weather turns cool in October and damages them, I put a call out on social media stating that they are available to the first takers to come get them.

I've had almost immediate success every year, with one person even driving forty miles round-trip to claim the bunch. Most recently, two of the ferns were taken so they could serve as backdrop decorations at an outdoor wedding; another went to live in a beautiful party barn.

We've easily and quickly given away two lawn mowers—one gone within two hours by doing nothing other than setting it at the end of our driveway with a FREE sign attached, and another, offered in a social media post.

And of course, you could have a garage sale, if that interests you. In my younger days, I had those every few years. I enjoyed visiting with shoppers as much as earning cash for my efforts. If or when we move from our current home, we may well have another such sale. In recent years, I've preferred other means of placing our unwanted goods.

Here are a few ideas how we can downsize some belongings and bless others in the process.

Old photos: We inherited pictures that our parents and other ancestors had kept since the 1800s. Unfortunately, if no one knew or thought to take the time to write the names of the people on the backs of these images, by the time we inherited them, no one remained who knew the IDs.

If I can't figure it out now through comparisons with other photos (I'm the last one remaining in my original immediate family), I don't see the point of keeping the pictures. But perhaps a library or historical society in the community where one's families lived might want them.

They might take them to document the history of buildings or vehicles in the background, the style of clothing, or other cultural reasons represented in the photos.

Other family members might like to have them with the idea that they can solve the identification mysteries, or, they might want to keep them anyway because they have been in the family archives for so long.

If family members aren't interested in the photos, and you can't quite allow yourself to lift the lid on the recycling bin, post them on social media inside talk-of-the-town-type groups in communities where the unknown people may have lived. Offer to give the photos away to anyone who wants them.

On one such social media group, I spotted a photo of someone's relative as a small girl on the back of a horse. Also in the photo, to my delight, appeared my father, as a boy of about twelve, leading the horse—his! I had never seen that photo before and got a kick out of the find.

Artsy-crafty friends might enjoy unidentified pictures for use in their artwork or handmade cards.

If you strike out all around, toss them and rest assured you've gone above and beyond in trying to find homes for the old images.

Cards and letters: My family saves cards from birthdays, anniversaries, sympathy, get well, some Christmas (but I usually dispose of those after the holiday), graduations, retirements, and births of children. There are graduation programs dating back generations, old marriage licenses, real estate deeds, and other miscellaneous papers.

It is wonderful to look through these papers before discarding them. Are there others in the extended family who might want to keep the cards to remember particular loved ones? They also might want to keep those vintage papers that signified the beginnings of marriages and families as well as homes and other properties.

As for letters, I have those dating back to fifth grade. Long letters and short notes are full of junior high angst and high school letters contain an advanced case of the same. There are entire friendships played out on either handwritten or typewritten pages filling envelopes, or folded with no envelope at all, before emails largely did away with such letters.

These communications could possibly provide means for reconnecting with friends or family members you no longer see nor write to. Ask them if they'd like to have the diary-like letters. I know that if someone asked if I wanted mine back, I'd happily take them. At the least, it's informative to reread and understand our thoughts as younger people.

When you think about it, most letters are more about what the writer is doing, thinking, and concerned with than about the recipient. It makes sense that they should have the letters back—if they want them—and if you don't.

It might lead to an enriched or renewed friendship. Or at least a pleasant lunch out catching up. It almost always seems to take a "reason" to get together with people after a long absence to keep it from feeling awkward.

Yearbooks or photo directories: Yearbooks consume a ton of storage space. We should know as we have them not only from our own and our sons' school days but from Brian's forty-year career working at schools. He wants to keep them all so we will.

But maybe you don't want to keep nor store the number of yearbooks on your shelves. Maybe you have a yearbook from your deceased relative's sophomore year of high school. His kids might adore having the keepsake. A library in the appropriate city or town would likely accept it.

There may be yearbooks that you don't have a close connection with but you hate to trash such nostalgic heirlooms. Many people might well love to get their hands on these. But how? Again, social media groups might be the ticket to making someone's day by handing off the yearbook.

Many high school classes have their own social media pages. It will probably take a lot less time than you think to connect with someone who could solve this particular storage problem.

Books and crafts supplies: Unwanted books and craft supplies can be helpful donations for schools, daycares, Sunday school classes or other venues that might use your children's books or general-interest volumes featuring animal photos or other educational pictures. Ask any teachers or daycare providers you know about sources that might want them.

Maybe a loved one left you with a box of books about zoo animals. Or trains. Or U.S. presidents. If you are on book-overload already, and perhaps those volumes aren't personal page-turners, consider giving them away to those who might use them.

You can likely always donate them to your favorite library where often the community's Friends of the Library or a similar group sponsors book sales to help finance library projects.

Or, is there a church or other general-interest garage sale planned? The sponsor likely welcomes the donation. An interior decorator might have a source who would like them for room staging.

When you're overly equipped: What to do with random equipment in your garage that is dated or maybe doesn't even work? Give it away.

Funny story: a whiz at repairing small engines, Brian's dad Ray also loved garage sales. Once we stopped at such a sale where he spotted a weed trimmer he wanted to check out. Here is our exchange:

"Does it work?" I asked.

"I hope not."

"Why do you say that?"

"So that I can get it cheaper."

He had confidence he could fix it and loved the thrill of a super-thrifty find. Often we might have similar things that otherwise end up in a landfill, but a local tinkerer might happily take them away—if we could find each other.

General merchandise: Many lack the inclination to personally place no-longer-wanted belongings. So, go with charitable or other organizations that will accept general merchandise. Clothing may be useful for those being released from incarceration. Animal shelters may welcome worn blankets, towels, and pillows.

If you prefer dropping things off at a particular charity, such as a homeless shelter or nonprofit's thrift shop, it's always best to contact such places in advance to see if there's an interest in and space for your things, and to schedule a drop. I've even had them pick up large items such as sofas that are in decent shape. Also, search to connect with online communities that sell or list free stuff.

The cliché that one person's trash is another person's treasure is as true today as ever.

When it comes to cleaning out the homestead, sometimes it's simply time to let go of things in whatever way you determine best; to free the space stuff takes in your attic, basement, drawers—and mind—by letting it go on to new lives of service.

23

Showers of memories

THERE ARE MANY REASONS that I love visiting my small, hometown church. Unfortunately, the years pass quickly, which means that sadly, funeral services have brought me there on occasion. Yet recent years have also meant happier times. I once provided the Brownsville alumni's annual-dinner program. There were luncheon presentations relating to my novels. Most recently came the joy of celebrating the hundredth birthday of Geneva, a beautiful, active member of the church who has been so all my life. (Since then, she has cleared another year!)

Inside the familiar building, I look around and see what others do not: my past. Scenes are played out from my entire life, from autumn Trick-or-Treat for UNICEF parties to summer vacation Bible schools, to Sunday school, dinners made and served by the Women's Society of Christian Service, later renamed United Methodist Women, to mother-daughter banquets. Not to mention our own wedding and reception.

I also think of the household-themed bridal showers. The church ladies organized showers for engaged girls in the community who were affiliated in some way with the church. During my girlhood I loved to attend with Mom and watch these young brides-to-be open their gifts while they stood behind the same wooden table still located in the building today.

Back then, I watched intently as a friend of the honoree whisked away the ribbons from those newly opened gifts to create a bow bouquet, threading the ribbon into slits scissored into a paper plate.

I don't know if this activity is only an old-fashioned Midwestern tradition, but the idea followed that the bride would carry the ribbon arrangement, instead of a formal floral bouquet, down the aisle during her wedding rehearsal. I wonder if many brides actually did this. I know of one friend who did. Does any young bride today know what I'm even talking about?

After a childhood spent attending bridal showers, the evening arrived for my own. I still have the list of those who attended and what they brought. This, at a time when you bought for people what you thought they needed, or maybe something that you personally recommended, "to start housekeeping," as Mom would say.

Her go-to shower gifts consisted of colorful, glass candy dishes from Hahn's Jewelry store in Liberty.

I wonder if Mom happened to be shopping for such a present on the day of President John F. Kennedy's assassination. We were inside that store when we heard the news on the radio.

AT MY BRIDAL SHOWER, the organizing committee of sweet church ladies gifted me with a silver-toned tray with wooden handles and a glass insert. I've used that gift many times for everything from a relish tray to the base for a candle centerpiece, and to my eyes, it looks elegant every time.

I still use the shiny, aluminum measuring cups and spoons from

Barb; the yellow Texas Ware mixing bowl from Cleo, and while cloth napkins don't get much time on our informal kitchen table, I have wooden napkin rings from Dorothy that await service when called to duty. I also have the yellow, electric hand-mixer from Steve and Linda. It still works like new on that increasingly rare occasion that I whip up a cake in my kitchen.

WHILE CLEANING THE ATTIC, I found a gift that had been missing for a long time: a small, original, landscape painting, the work of Gladys Rude, an artist of local renown. It's now propped against books on our bookcase.

Other thoughtful presents were appreciated, such as Vivian's round, hand-braided, blue-toned rag rug, and a small electric skillet. White dishes with 1970s gold-hued accents are no longer with us, having been replaced through the years.

I've never forgotten those lovely rites of passage when a young woman felt loved, cared for, and part of something special: a community of women who took an interest to invest in her.

There are charms of big-city life, many of which allude me since I've never lived in a large, urban setting; but this, a special gathering of women you've known your whole life, is a small-town delight, a demonstration of when your people rise up to wish you well. They take an evening of their time to eat cake and sip punch spiked with soda pop; mints and nuts on the side; everything accented in your chosen colors.

As the recipient of such caring, you wouldn't be happier in a grand hotel in the heart of New York City, nor seated at a noted café in Paris, France. At your own shower, you feel warm and valued. You are cheered on, seen, and encouraged.

MY MOTHER'S BRIDAL SHOWER took place approaching nine decades ago in the home of the bride-to-be's new mother-in-law, my eventual Grandma Jobe, with seventy-seven attending.

I found a stack of small cards that accompanied the gifts, the bunch tied with a bit of pink-and-white ribbon. The cards contain surnames still recognizable in the community; names you would likely still find on local school rosters and home deeds.

At Mom's 1934 shower, the gifts she unwrapped remain surprisingly typical of what a bride might receive today. There's an electric mixer—which would be the only mixer she ever used in her 58-year marriage. The most-duplicated gifts included: dishes (fourteen of them); pans (eight); towels and wash cloths (six of each); tea kettles (three); two pitchers, and a cake-pan set.

She also received a cookie jar, double boiler, rolling pin, ricer, skillet-and-tray combo, skillet alone, and this combination, which I found unique—an egg beater and cookie tray.

Today such items would not likely be bought twice due to modern, bridal registry wish lists. The shopper tends to shuffle through digital pages listing potential gifts in every price range so not to double-up on prior purchases. Electronic updates are made as each gift is bought.

However, the actual items needed to make a house tick boil down today, at least in part, to dishes, towels, and the occasional use of an electric mixer—the kinds of things that my mother and I both received all those decades ago.

Purposes of bridal showers were then, as they remain now: a chance to celebrate love, marriage, the possibilities of a long-and-happy life together, and all good things that come with those ideals. Plus, there's the opportunity to giggle, even roar with laughter, chat with your friends—and delight in those interesting-and-useful presents.

I think of the scripture: *Treat older women as you would your mother, and treat younger women with all purity as you would your own sisters.*—1 Timothy 5:2 (NLT)

I'll keep my mother's gift tags, the name of each giver on one side of each tag, the type of present on the other. Where does one properly store such a keepsake? Since I have no idea, they will stay inside my home, in a drawer of Grandma Jobe's buffet. That same buffet was no doubt inside Grandma's house the day of the shower.

Although the era of the standard community-wide, church-sponsored bridal shower may have passed from small towns, there remains something timeless about such an event. A bridal shower of any kind fills us with hope and good cheer.

Edythe Kaper wrote on the back of her gift card to my mother, "Best wishes for a long, happy married life."

Then she sealed that thought—with a baking dish.

24

Shelf life

ONCE UPON A TIME, friend Gay and I helped a mutual friend set up a yard sale. Gay opened one of the books destined for a price sticker and to everyone's amazement—especially the book owner's—there appeared a fifty-dollar bill. Delighted by the find, the owner used the cash to treat her helpers to a late-night pizza run.

While large denominations of cash, or any money at all, may or not be typical finds inside books passed down in a family, don't write it off. You just don't know what you'll see tucked between those pages. Before donating, selling, or even reshelving old volumes, consider taking the time to first flip through them.

Also, you may not want to keep the books, but you might find what previous owners wrote or placed inside them to be priceless— or at least interesting.

I have two old Bibles that belonged to my mother. The 1942 *King James'* black-leather cover is badly frayed, making me curious how it came to get into that poor a condition. Curiously, the inside pages and binding are in excellent shape. The book contains beautiful colored pictures depicting biblical stories.

Mom also used this particular Bible as a place to record family marriages and births. Traditionally, Bibles are great sources for handwritten genealogical records such as these. Be sure to check them out before ever discarding a Bible.

There's a similar situation with Brian's mother's Bible, dated 1954, where she also recorded marriages, and births of children, and grandchildren.

I also have a more recent Bible of my mother's. This hardcover is one that she appears to have used regularly in her studies as there are a number of yellow-highlighted passages.

But for me, even more significant are scriptures handwritten inside the cover. Mom put them down for her own reference—and now they are there for mine. And of course, they remain timeless and instructive.

Inside are newspaper clippings. There are the late evangelist Billy Graham's newspaper columns, and even Brian's and my wedding write-up from a local newspaper. I could remove all these things and put them elsewhere, but I choose to leave them where Mom placed them.

I have a row of vintage family Bibles which I keep side-by-side inside my glass-fronted antique bookcase.

I write and highlight inside my own Bible. I hope that it, too, will be a legacy for family members when I'm gone.

Do you know anyone who takes highlighting and underlining a step further in this way? By adding notes and dates of specific life situations next to scriptures that provide comfort and instruction? What a way to live a life in active relationship with the Lord, with an almost-diary-type record.

THERE'S A CLYDESDALE IN THE ATTIC

THROUGH THE YEARS, I'VE weeded out my collection of commercial cookbooks, but there are two I planned to always keep, one a hardcover, the other soft, both country recipe books. I intended to save them for no other reason than they were on my mother's shelves before they came to reside on mine. I also keep her church cookbooks and a large collection of recipes written out on cards and clipped from newspapers and magazines. I have similar files of recipes from Brian's mom, Mary.

Yet here's how time gets away. My mother's hardcover country cookbook, for example, has been in print since 1961. I've had since then to crack it open—and haven't. Until recently.

Not even looking for a recipe or seeking a trip down memory lane, I only wanted to use the cookbook in staging. I sought to redo the contents of the tiered shelving alongside our kitchen cabinets. I looked for some cookbook props with sizes that would fit the narrow shelf space.

When I took the sun-faded dust jacket off Mom's book, it suddenly looked as though it could have been published yesterday: pristine, crisp, and with an attractive red spine that would go well on the shelf.

But what I found inside the cover turned out to be the real gift: an envelope taped to the inside blank cover page holding clipped recipes from magazines for such dishes as fruit squares and beef stew. The outside of the envelope contains Mom's own personal table of contents for recipes that stood out to her.

There's one for a lard crust, not a recipe you see much these days. Still, it's what my mother used for pie crusts and in my growing-up years, we always kept on hand a large tin canister of lard. And you can bet that it makes one delicious crust. I'm sure Mom knew the recipe by heart.

Inside, Mom paperclipped a section of pages together. There's no comment, so I don't know what that means, but I'm leaving the clip there.

I've found this true when it comes to family Bibles—be sure

to look inside them for all manner of information tucked here and there about marriages, births, deaths, and clipped obituaries. There are other little surprises such as articles and poems that your ancestors thought enough of to save.

When I need a Mom fix, I'll look inside the cover of her books and see my mother's distinctive handwriting. Mom, who passed away at ninety-two, would be 108 the year I'm writing this.

As for the second cookbook, I saved it all these years. Upon closer inspection, I noticed something odd that I had never observed over all these years. It is actually a paperback version of the hardcover. Could it be that copy belonged to my grandmother? Why Mom had both is yet another unsolved mystery.

I wonder what everyday mysteries you and I will leave behind for our loved ones.

25

Leaving us in stitches

BECAUSE I CAME ALONG later in my parents' lives, it often seems that I've missed out on experiences that my contemporaries enjoyed. There were no siblings my age, and numerous events of family lore had long-since taken place, leaving me with other people's stories of memories from special occasions rather than my own. But most of all, I never got to meet three of four grandparents. They passed on before I came along.

All that contributes, I suppose, to my special appreciation for storytelling, enjoying insights into the history of family heirlooms, and the saving of all kinds of relics. Plus, I don't like to miss a thing.

Whereas Dad is an only child, his one sibling passing in infancy, Mom came from a large family. She inherited few belongings of her mother's, but one of those is Edith Jarrett's lacy, taupe tablecloth.

On Sundays, my parents didn't work, even around the house. Dad took the day off from whatever farming needed done other than what became necessary. He took a leisurely Sunday-morning bath, then often pursued some type of activity around the house from reading his art books, to dabbling with his acrylic paints, to if company came, playing croquet on the portion of our lawn that we dubbed, "The Croquet Yard."

My folks also liked a card game called "500" and took every opportunity to enjoy that if another card-playing twosome showed up. Dad's favorite of all the games, however, was chess, and he relished a chance to play with anyone who knew how—or wanted to learn.

EVERY SUNDAY OF THE twenty years I lived at home, and those that came after that when I didn't, the *good* tablecloth came out, the one my mother inherited, covering the kitchen table with what I interpreted as elegance. It replaced, if only for the day, the seasonal plastic one that covered the table on weekdays.

Mom nearly always made a nicer noon meal on Sundays, and I can still mentally conjure the scent of a beef roast in the oven when entering the house after church. The nice tablecloth came out after the meal and stayed the rest of the day.

When my folks' things were divided, this tablecloth went home with my brother and sister-in-law, Tim and Jeannie.

For one of our boys' high school open houses, I asked to borrow it, and Jeannie graciously said yes—then told me to keep it. Now in my house, my maternal grandmother's tablecloth comes out for special occasions—but no longer every Sunday. I need to wash it, yet thankfully, almost as if by force of will, it remains beautiful as it is, delaying what could be its demise should I attempt its laundering.

After all, I already nearly ruined another beautiful tablecloth, this one custom-ordered for our dining room table from Beverly Walcott, master-craftswoman of the crochet hook. I learned of her talent while interviewing her about another skill set, that of thrifty living, and her particular techniques.

We sat for the interview at a table covered in the most beautiful, intricately crocheted tablecloth I had ever seen. It turns out she crocheted it.

"I could make one for you," she offered.

A few short weeks later, she delivered the reasonably priced beige handiwork for our dining-room table to my work desk. It washes like a dream, despite my nearly wrecking the beauty.

One time I washed it—and got a dreadful surprise. To my shock, I lifted from the washer a pink tablecloth! Something red had been placed in the machine and took a spin with my beautiful, handmade work of art. I decided to bleach it and see if it would remove the pink. To my astonishment, it did, and turned the original beige tablecloth a sparkling white.

The white goes beautifully in our home, matching the woodwork, looking as though it has always been white.

That tablecloth dresses our dining-room table almost all the time, except when it goes with me on the road somewhere to cover my book-sales table.

One day while set up at a small-town festival, I thought I had a certain book sale! The potential customer kept eyeing my table from a distance. At times such as that, the author's mind wanders: maybe she has a book club and will buy enough copies for everyone; perhaps she wants to ask about a speaking engagement. Could be, she simply would like a signed copy for herself. I smiled her way as she got close and bolted toward my table. I straightened up with anticipation.

"Your tablecloth is *gorgeous*," she said, beaming. "Where did you get it?"

Not the first time I had heard that. And not the only time the table covering appeared more interesting to the shopper than did the books stacked on it.

THIRD OF MY KEEPABLE tablecloths is also courtesy of Jeannie, who thoughtfully gave me a white butterfly-themed one that belonged to one of our community's elder stateswomen from my growing-up years.

Jeannie picked it up at the home of Ray and Cleo Winters at their estate sale. If that tablecloth could talk, I can only imagine how it would speak of the delicious meals that Cleo prepared for Ray from their Brownsville home of decades. Or, maybe she prepared her adult Sunday school lessons on top of it. Mom marveled at Cleo's knowledge of scriptures.

Cleo had given me a Texas Ware mixing bowl as a bridal gift, and I continue to use that yellow-speckled bowl often, as I have throughout our marriage. It's no worse for the wear, either. I saw one like it in an antiques store. It is a strange feeling the first time you see that something you were given as a wedding present is now considered an antique.

INVITED TO PROVIDE A library program to a regional quilting club, I decided to decorate the table with my prized quilt that belonged to Grandma Jobe. The striking quilt has likely never seen actual use as it is in perfect condition with blue-green and cream borders and brightly colored puffy flowers that are always blooming on each block. The quilt is seventy-five years if it's a day.

I thought maybe bringing the old quilt would strike these master quilters as me trying too hard, and not be of much interest. To my delighted surprise, the women fawned over it, examining the stitches, and one suggested that its pattern be that for their next year's club quilt.

They invited me to join the organization! There were even offers to help teach me how to quilt. While tempted by their welcoming gestures, I remembered my lack of sewing talent. I'll have to pass, and resume playing with words.

I thoroughly enjoyed the evening with the group, however, and certainly can see the attraction to both quilting and the gathering of quilters.

A COUSIN TO THE quilt is the comforter. The difference between the two is that comforter fabric is tied off and secured with yarn instead of stitched with thread. Brian had no problem with me creating Christmas stockings from one of his grandmother's comforters, cutting it up and sewing the pieces by hand into spacious stockings. This is the kind of sewing I like, that which is more craft than tailored outfit or pieced quilt.

I took the completed stockings to a shop that boasted a fancy machine that embroidered the recipients' names and years of birth onto them. I only wish I had additional pieces of this comforter to create more stockings for any incoming in-laws and the next generation of Cronks.

While I foolishly never think to wear them, or they somehow seem too important for my ordinary meal preps, a number of pretty calico and other cheerful, cotton aprons fill a section of my kitchen Sellers Cabinet.

Mom made one apron with leftover fabric from a skirt she sewed for me in elementary school. There's my little 4-H apron and scarf—neither of which I wore beyond the dress review. But wouldn't they be adorable on a special little girl today?

OF ALL THE THINGS we regularly use in our home, the oldest from our marriage is the multi-hued, blue throw that Jeannie's mother made for me as a Christmas gift in 1976. It started out inside my hope chest but didn't stay there long because I called it into service. It remains fabulously warm and wonderful.

It has been a workhorse in our family for all of the forty-some years of our marriage. It has offered comfort and warmth to babies and toddlers, teens, and adults alike. And it washes like a dream to do it all over again the next time.

Recently our son Sam's bulldog, Jax, spotted the bright-blue blanket folded on a seldom-used chair in our living room. After eyeing it for a moment, Jax jumped onto the throw, circled himself repeatedly until he had it just right, then plopped down for a snooze.

"Look, Sam," I said. "Jax loves the blue afghan!"

"Every Cronk loves the blue afghan," he said.

He's not wrong.

26

Not much of a spice girl
(And a reader challenge)

SURELY IT HADN'T BEEN *that* long ago since I went through our kitchen spice drawer to sort and clean it out. Yet what I found in that drawer full of small jars speaks otherwise. That, or I did a terrible job. Probably both.

The ground nutmeg's expiration date came and went in June 2019. The ground mustard expired five months before that. But those are nothing compared to the ground cloves and whole allspice which gave up the ghost in 2009—twelve years before I tossed them. *How could that be?* I wondered, feeling the role of the most-inept homemaker possible, the antithesis of Becky Homecy.

I'm being utterly transparent here; revealing my lack of sophistication along with possession of a most *common* palate to say this, but here we go: I don't find that one-fourth a teaspoon of anything I've ever driven to the store to buy amounts to, as Mom would say, "a hill of beans" regarding any recipe prepared inside my kitchen.

I dare say that I could go the rest of my life without a jar of cardamon expiring in my cabinet and never look back. Maybe you've bought an herb or spice for a recipe that caught your eye that required a pinch or sprinkle, then you never used it again.

The coriander? Now that's one I didn't buy for a recipe, but rather, out of curiosity. I read that the ancient Israelites' manna in the desert is said to have resembled coriander seed, only white. I wanted to taste it out of sheer wonder. I'm simply intrigued with the whole concept of manna from heaven and how God provided it daily for forty years.

I hope when I get to heaven, at the welcome reception, the servers will pass around platters of finger food featuring manna. (You think I'm kidding.) Okay, I am somewhat obsessed with that heavenly sustenance.

The herbs and spices that I actually do use, and regularly, are garlic, onion, cinnamon, chili powder, salt, and pepper.

I TOOK EVERYTHING OUT of the spice drawer, then consolidated containers of toothpicks. I placed as many as would fit into a pretty glass toothpick holder that had belonged to Brian's mother. I washed down and dried the drawer's interior, then tossed the outdated herbs and spices.

The few remaining flavor enhancers are those that I use regularly enough to justify setting aside a small drawer for them, and there's some breathing room for newcomers. I wonder: Is an expiration date of, say, April 2020 all that bad?

Oh, don't worry; I'll be sure to keep checking those labels much more closely before anything is served to company or prepared for a pitch-in. Oh, all right, family members, that includes cooking for you, too.

Now I have a challenge for you, dear reader. Drop what you're doing and go check out your own spice rack or drawer. What did you find?

I'll wait here for your answer …

Surprising, isn't it?

27

Christmas trees tell stories of our lives

WHEN THE HOLIDAYS ARRIVE, the sixty-something me would like to have a little talk with the younger version, the one who bought the nine-feet-tall artificial Christmas tree a dozen years ago. Back then, it seemed like a great idea. What was she thinking?

Why not go even bigger and get a twelve-footer? That's what she thought. Thank heaven she (the younger me) didn't act on those thoughts. A nine-footer is more than enough, thank you.

Christmas trees have always been a big deal in my world. I grew up near Wolfe's Christmas Tree Farm. What a treat to pick out a real evergreen before we began using an artificial version. A favorite day of the year involved putting up the tree. It remains a special one on the calendar now during the Thanksgiving weekend, but the truth is, anymore I'm glad once the chore, er, *fun* is complete.

Is there a more important question to consider when buying a home than if there's a great spot for the Christmas tree?

145

The first gift that Brian and I received as a couple were pewter Christmas ornaments, each hanging from red yarn. Brian had loaned his decorated tree to Mary, owner of the spacious home where he rented the upstairs apartment, during the first Christmas of our relationship. For whatever reason, she hadn't put one up that year on the main floor, and asked if she could borrow his when she hosted her family's celebration.

As a thank you for the loan, she gave him those ornaments in seasonal shapes of an angel, bell, stocking, and dove. They've been on our tree every year since.

In the early 1980s, as a full-time college student, I picked up a couple adorable handmade ornaments at a campus Christmas bazaar. One is a felt mouse, nestled inside half a walnut shell, swinging from thread. The other is a sled made of frozen treat sticks. Both look as good as the day I bought them.

THROUGHOUT OUR MARRIAGE, EVERY time we take a vacation, mostly to historic sites throughout the country, I pick up ornaments from such places as Thomas Jefferson's Monticello, George Washington's Mount Vernon, the Gerald Ford and JFK libraries, and the Empire State Building, plus countless more.

The late 1980s saw the start of a long-running collection of Hallmark ornaments for our sons. Each year the boys and I looked over the crop of ornaments where they then selected which one each son wanted to add to his collection.

We've now given those decorations to them for their own trees. However, I retained one that represents one of the two happiest moments of Brian's and my lives: when we became parents.

Along with that ornament, another favorite is an ordinary, gold-hued glass ball that had belonged to my folks. On it, brother Tim drew a picture of the Brownsville covered bridge in black marker. The functional bridge served as a landmark near our farm for one hundred thirty years, was disassembled, sold, and is now gracing the beautiful Mill Race Park in Columbus, Indiana.

The decoration brings back memories of riding the school bus through that bridge, and how in the third grade, as soon as we came through it, I looked down and noticed red spots all over my arms: measles! We rode our ponies through that bridge. It is a landmark of my growing-up years and I went through that bridge nearly every day of my youth.

Another favorite decoration is a whimsical, felt gingerbread man. It's a reminder of Julie, the first friend I made when we moved to our community. I didn't know a soul here, and she took me under her wing in a Madison County Extension Homemakers Club called the Willing Owl Workers.

A unique ornament I picked up on my trip of a lifetime to Israel is a camel with this on it: Trust God but tie up your camel.

A teacher colleague of Brian's gifted him an ornament she must have looked high and low to find. It's an angel playing an accordion—a nod to a childhood hobby that surprises everyone he knows—himself included, I think.

AS ORNAMENT STORIES GO, the felted dove, the symbol of peace, comes with one I can't forget. On a bus tour in Washington, D.C., our group visited the home of former President Woodrow Wilson. It's a detailed tour with mostly all original Wilson furnishings intact—so many that it seems the family had merely stepped out for a bit while we were there.

At the end of the tour, some of us visited the house museum's gift shop. I've never met a gift shop I didn't like, so naturally, I looked around with an eye out for themed Christmas ornaments.

I came across what appeared as a garland of doves, packaged inside tightly wrapped plastic. A price tag affixed to the outer wrapper read twelve dollars. Oh, yes. That would go home with me! My mind exploded with ideas: I could use that garland on our tree, over a doorway, or on a wreath. Thrilled with my keepsake, I paid for it, and headed happily to the bus to wait while the others finished shopping.

While waiting, I unwrapped the package to check out the garland's length. To my shock, it wasn't a garland at all! Instead, a flock of about a dozen doves fell out, each one on a thread hanger. Suddenly, I knew that the doves were not twelve bucks for the package—but twelve bucks *apiece*. Evidently the employee stocking the shelves had accidentally left out the whole package before unwrapping the single dove ornaments.

I ran off the bus back to the gift shop and quickly explained what had happened. I told them I would only be keeping one dove—the one I paid for. I'm not sure that the clerk understood what had happened, but I knew, and sprinted back to the bus so not to miss my ride.

How horrifying to realize that however inadvertent—I could have been nabbed for shoplifting from U.S. President Wilson!

IN A RECENT YEAR, friend Gay gifted me with a small lidded-jar tree decoration containing tiny white lights that lit a small woodland scene. I gaze into that itsy-bitsy world on a chilled winter's night and feel cozy and warm.

This isn't to mention the sheep ornaments I've collected for most of our marriage. They have their own tree, a flocked version that I put up in the dining room. Friends continue to gift me with unique sheep when I least expect it. There are probably one hundred or more sheep on the tree, each one ewe-nique. (Sorry. Kind of.)

It appears that many decorations which adorn our family Christmas tree are secular. Many have nothing directly to do with honoring the birth of the Christ Child.

Yet our ornaments are symbolic of the lives we live. They represent the gratitude felt as Christians, for the experiences and places we go, and the people God has blessed us with along life's way. I love to stare at our lit-up trees on a December night, and think about all that.

At a time when we're trying to pare down and clean out, the ornaments that represent the stories of our lives aren't going anywhere. Themed trees that coordinate with a specific décor are beautiful. We are a sentimental lot, though, and simply don't wish to part with our miscellaneous collection of ornaments.

But that nine-feet-tall tree? When the day comes to replace it, a much smaller one will be selected. The ornaments will simply have to snuggle closer—much like those doves inside that package.

28

The prodigy

A S A KINDERGARTEN STUDENT in Mrs. Brown's class, Brian painted a picture that drew attention. Not on the classroom bulletin board, but in a national exhibit sponsored by The Smithsonian Institution.

Brian painted *My Street is Snowy* in watercolors for entry into the *Third Biennial Exhibition of American Child Art*.

Students in thirty-nine states submitted, probably through their schools, more than ten thousand pieces in the competition. The field narrowed to one hundred paintings for the show. One of those belonged to Brian. We recently unearthed a 1959 publication of *Arts and Activities: The Teacher's Arts and Crafts Guide*, which shows the winning pictures in black and white.

Pretty heady stuff for a little boy from Riley Elementary School in Hammond, Indiana.

Or maybe for his parents, anyway. I'm not sure Brian thought much about it at the time.

The paintings were on display first at the Galerie St. Etienne in New York City. After that, the exhibit toured the country in major museums, galleries, and schools, according to Brian's certificate, which I recently framed and placed on the wall in our study.

With such talent on display at age five, where could this lead? Brian's folks planned to find out. They bought their son art supplies to develop his skills. What parents wouldn't think that if their child's name appeared in the same sentence with "Smithsonian," "painting," and "tour," it was the start of something big?

Maybe he'll become a famous artist or art teacher. Could be he'll follow in the footsteps of his Aunt Janis and become a commercial artist. How special to find your place in the art world before you know your times tables, or even know that times tables are a thing.

The problem, though, is that Brian was done.

His art career had been bright, but brief. Apparently the inspiration of his own snowy street had been all he had in him regarding the life of an artist.

Yet that wasn't the end of his artistic endeavors. A few years later, for reasons he still doesn't understand, let alone explain to inquiring minds, Brian started taking accordion lessons. Maybe his parents figured that their certificate-wielding son had moved on toward an interest in the musical arts.

They could work with that. With five dollars down and a payment plan, they purchased a student accordion for five hundred fifty dollars. By my calculations, that's a bundle of money, let alone for a typical family's 1960s budget.

BRIAN DOESN'T SAY MUCH about his musical instruction other than his oft-repeated quote, "When I had to miss baseball practice for a lesson, that ended it. No more accordion."

He never became a professional baseball player, either, but he still loves the sport. While it's true that he also enjoys listening to music, especially classic-rock tunes from the 1960s and '70s, his interest in the accordion is, shall we say, minimal?

The accordion topic usually comes up at family reunions. It seems that his short-lived pursuits as both an artist and musician have become that of family lore, and speaking of either gets a few predictable laughs. For some reason, Brian doesn't much enjoy talking about his early exploration of the arts.

That's why I'm floored whenever we prepare for a trip to Washington, D.C., because I know this is coming: "Wonder if the Smithsonian still has my painting."

Really? I can't believe he would ask that. But he's not joking.

I tell him it's not possible that the Smithsonian would have kept his kindergarten painting. It's not reasonable to imagine that his picture is temperature-controlled at taxpayers' expense inside an archive deep within our nation's capital.

He's not even listening.

"Wonder how I'd find out if they have it," he says, undeterred.

The Smithsonian is America's attic, cataloging and displaying such national treasures as Dorothy's ruby slippers, moon rocks, and—*My Street is Snowy?* I don't think so.

THE ACCORDION CASE IS heavy. How a little kid could manage toting the thing around is a mystery.

Brian's plan during our cleaning-out period included wrestling it down from the attic and figuring out what to do with it. So far all he figures is to keep it in his closet. Online he found an Indy music store that accepts instruments, and we thought maybe we'd drive down one of these days and see if they'll buy it.

This must be the sort of thing one does when reaching advanced senior citizenship. If the sale goes through, maybe to celebrate, we'll use part of the proceeds to split a hamburger and salad from the early-bird menu somewhere on the way home. Sound about right?

Recently son Ben and his childhood-neighbor pal, Randall, stopped by. Ben wanted to show Randall his father's extensive collection of original, classic-rock vinyl albums. The boys cranked up the volume on Brian's stereo. I told Randall about the accordion that we planned to sell. He asked to see it.

"You *can't* get rid of this!" the friend pleaded, enchanted by a vintage instrument that you don't see much of in central Indiana. We begged Brian to play us a tune, but the best he would do consisted of pulling on the straps as I grabbed a quick photo for posterity.

Due to the encouragement, I don't think Brian's accordion is going anywhere. If that makes him happy, it makes me happier still.

However, the question remains: What happened to *My Street is Snowy*?

The other day I mentioned to Brian that I planned to write about his art for this book. He told me that he took a closer look at his information about the old exhibit. He no longer believes that the Smithsonian has his painting.

Well now, he's come to his senses, I thought.

That's not it.

"I wonder if that museum in New York City has it," he deadpanned.

"I don't think they would have it," I answered.

"What would they have done with it?" he asked.

"They probably returned it," I responded. "Or threw it out."

"They didn't send it back," he said with certainty. "They wouldn't have thrown it out."

We're talking about 1959 here.

If we ever again make it to New York City, I think we should visit the Galerie St. Etienne. We should take along Brian's certificate, the awards magazine, and ask if they have any idea if *My Street is Snowy* is in their archives. I could even pull the "Do you know who this man is?" card, referencing my own resident artist.

Sounds unlikely, ridiculous even, to consider such a thing. But the uncanny truth about Brian Cronk is that sometimes, he's right about the oddest things.

And, if they simply stare at us blankly, which I suspect they will, right before showing us the door, we'll kindly pause outside long enough for a photo. I'll ask him to hold his kindergarten certificate. He'll roll his eyes.

I'll say, "We're not leaving without a photo."

After all, that's where my artist got his start.

29

Mothers are keepers

INSIDE MY JEWELRY BOX are two precious rings. One of the gold-tone bands contains a glass "sapphire," the other, a glass "ruby."

These rings have never been worn in public. What makes them priceless, although not in a monetary sense, is that Ben bought them for me on two occasions. They were purchased during annual elementary school fundraisers.

One ring came inside a green box shaped like a frog; the other in a clear, plastic square. When presented with them, I thanked my little boy, then promptly tucked away the jewels for safe keeping. I knew that if I wore them even once, then forgot and ran them under water, the metal might tarnish or the stones pop out. So, just to be safe, I kept them in the back of my jewelry box, and didn't give them much added thought.

Ben had grown up by the time he surprised me with the question, "Mom, why didn't you ever wear those rings I bought you?"

Years had passed, but he hadn't forgotten, and he seemed a bit sad.

How can a mother save so many things that belong to her children, yet get something so wrong as those small rings? I should have worn them out rather than put them away out of sight and mind.

The age-old dilemma rages on between preserving a keepsake versus using it even if it gets damaged or used up.

MOMS TEND TO BE KEEPERS. Not all, of course, but I know a good number of them. We want to remember our children's young lives, and we archive choice pieces as visuals to preserve and touch.

If our sons received school certificates, I saved them; if they got perfect scores on their homework, or wrote stories bound with brass clamps securing the pages, they are inside my attic. Yes, even now.

If you're an adult child of one of these keeper-moms, and wondering what happened to all the yearbooks you tirelessly paged through, memorizing names of all the students in your entire school—ask your mother; she's likely got them put up somewhere safe—if she's like me and can only remember where that might be!

We have our grandparents' high school graduation programs in pristine condition, thanks to *their* mothers who no doubt carefully carried them home from the ceremonies and archived them.

Could these ancestors have imagined that their great-granddaughter would view these more than a century later? I don't suppose that was ever considered. They just knew they wanted to hold special moments in paper form, in the only tangible means available then.

I attended a family baby shower where the mother-to-be opened a box from her mother-in-law. Swathed in tissue paper, out came a beautiful handmade blanket that the new baby's father had used as an infant. That day it passed to the next generation. Both mother-in-law and daughter-in-law wept with joy.

Aside from the usual dresser-drawer contents of scarves, socks, and undies, I keep a stash—"the best of" Mother's Day and birthday cards that Brian and our boys have given me through the years. Pretty flowers on the front don't matter so much as the sweet notes and touching sentiments handwritten inside.

I can re-read a card that's been kept next to my heart—or next to my flannel pajamas—which is kind of like my heart.

AFTER MONTHS SPENT PARING down, we've got the attic in pretty good shape. Curiously, though, we retain custody of a good number of our sons' childhood belongings.

There are totes of memorable baby clothes, Scouts-and-sports-team uniforms. There are containers of elementary school art projects and those particular papers with stickers or perfect scores.

There are some specialty items, such as senior gifts that are so specific to the moment, I don't see anyone, not even this fan mom, displaying them in a "den," as is often the suggestion for such things. Sam's framed award for winning his school's geography bee and band awards, as well as oodles of Ben's baseball trophies, are stashed away.

Right about now, some of you are squirming in your seat, wanting to ask what in the dickens I'm thinking. *Why*, you may wonder, *are you still sheltering all their stuff?*

Hold the phone! I hear you, but here's why.

Although grown and on their own, our sons remain young enough that these belongings haven't reached treasure status. But the other, more practical reason, is that at the time of this writing, neither son is in his long-term home. Neither has the space necessary to store several big plastic tubs of random memory items that don't currently interest them.

Plus, why move something a time or two or three before they care about these things? They are welcome to take away their goods any time they wish. And if they don't wish before the time comes that we move and can no longer keep them, they will then *need* to make some decisions. *Their decisions.*

AS FOR THE SENTIMENTAL heirlooms we're keeping, as well as generations of family photos that are tucked away, we can do our kids and future generations favors by labeling everything now. Include names of people and locations on each image. If we don't identify people in the pictures, my guess is that the photos will be thrown out.

I've mentioned how at times regarding our old photos, everyone has passed on who could identify them. Recently, a friend discussed upgrading her cellphone and that during the transition, she lost a large number of photos of her granddaughter.

Our phones contain pictures documenting our lives and those of our nearest-and-dearest loved ones. We continue to take images as though we are covering our own and their lives for a documentary. Often, many of these will not make it to physical copies.

Entire childhoods' worth of photo memories, not to mention other special occasions, and everyday life, may be lost in cyberspace.

Consider printing copies of those images in case there's a glitch with cyberspace storage.

I also notice that while people show hundreds, even thousands of photos of their children and grandchildren via social media, there are often few pictures of those kids inside the context of their surroundings, nor with extended-family members.

You are documenting their lives not only for social media acknowledgment, but for the future. The context of your family members' lives—the rooms they lived in, how the Christmas tree looked, what food Grandma served on Easter—may in the long run be of great interest.

CONSIDER ARCHIVING YOUR STUFF. You may want to put together a notebook—simple, or fancy—whatever your style. Inside it tell what you know about your keepsake belongings. Take photos of the objects you save that come with family stories—simple, kinfolk tales such as those I share in this book. Remember, it's your story to tell. Who will tell it if you don't?

Who among us has a trunk that came over with our ancestors to America or a suitcase from another country toted through Ellis Island? Few, I suppose. But that doesn't mean your humble belongings aren't special to your families and will be to descendants to come.

My parents had a pair of small, oval tea tables made of curly maple. One of those sat for many years in an alcove next to my childhood bedroom. It came time to divide their things among family members.

In picking up one of the tables, we learned that it contained a handmade wooden latch on the bottom. In releasing it, the tabletop dropped—thus, a drop-leaf table. More than that, a note underneath one of those tables fell from yellowed tape. We have no idea how long it had been there, penned by my late father. It reads in part:

"I wasn't over 10 or 12 when these stands were made by an old man in Liberty. If I remember right, he made these stands free of charge for lumber from this tree. I do remember going to Liberty with Dad and Uncle Bert in our Model T Coupe to see the finished wood and how they carried on about it. I remember it just looked like wood to me, but the old woodworker wanted them to see if they could find more lumber from that tree. It sounded silly to me."

The memory would be from between 1922 and 1924.

I have both tables. Originally Tim and I each had one but he gave me his. They are sweet heirlooms, made loads more special with our father's note.

ALONG WITH THE HEIRLOOMS and photos, in practical terms, do your kids or other close descendants know where your important papers are kept? Your will, insurance policies, titles to property, and vehicles? What about paperwork pertaining to regular household bills and how to deal with them?

It's a retirement goal to get all that together, the whole works regarding the business side of our belongings and our lives, and to do it in a succinct way that's easy to navigate.

And then there's the elephant in the room. Do those who will carry out your final wishes *know* your final wishes? Do *you* know your final wishes?

Do you want a funeral? What kind? Do you own a cemetery plot? Where's the deed? It could be that your funeral expenses have been paid for but if your next of kin doesn't know that, and the details, what a shame if they paid for another funeral.

If these important papers are stored in a bank lockbox, discuss with the bank what is involved in adding another name to the identity card for admittance into that box. Make sure the person behind that name knows where the key is kept and where the box is located.

Be sure to have a will, and if you have one, keep it current and located where your loved ones can get to it.

Something I plan to add to that last-will-and-testament packet is a personal farewell letter to my loved ones. In it I want my spouse and children to have no doubt about how much I love them. I plan to also leave no speculation about my beliefs and my Christian faith. And I will leave them with my deepest request: that the one thing they can do for *me* and more importantly for *themselves*, is to make sure they end up in heaven.

Consider 3 John 4 (NLT): *I could have no greater joy than to hear that my children are following the truth.*

Sometimes we fail to share with those we love most what means the most to us in the lives we live. We can also leave them with that information. And, of course they will read it.

30

---❖❖❖---

Thoughts and prayers

SOMETHING I HAVEN'T MENTIONED is what our family went through during the writing of this book. We dealt with a cancer diagnosis. When I say we, it's because cancer, as with any major disease or illness, affects the whole family and web of friendships, not only the person going through the ordeal.

In our case, it's Brian who suffered the diagnosis, and over several months, which in some ways seem like several years, underwent chemotherapy, treatments from those complications, then major surgery, and healing.

From the start, the cavalry arrived from several different outposts in our lives. Some quite unexpected.

The first to show up appeared from the archives of our lives on the very day Brian received the diagnosis. Earlier in the week I had a rare email conversation with Wes, the first publisher who ever hired me, then hired me again after his promotion to another newspaper across state. While our discussion centered on current events—what he didn't know until I told him—was that *my* current event concerned Brian's biopsy, the results coming due that Friday. I asked for prayer.

That Friday, Wes and wife Kay called. The Holy Spirit had directed Kay to give Brian a message about his diagnosis and share some scripture. It was an incredible phone call, with 1 Peter 2:24 highlighted, along with Psalm 107, emphasis on verses 6 and 20, along with Psalm 91.

Across the miles, the four of us prayed together on the phone. These are the scriptural selections Kay felt led to share with us:

He personally carried our sins in his body on the cross so that we can be dead to sin and live for what is right. By his wounds you are healed.—1 Peter 2:24 (NLT).

"LORD, help!" they cried in their trouble, and he rescued them from their distress.—Psalm 107:6 (NLT).

He sent out his word and healed them, snatching them from the door of death.—Psalm 107:20 (NLT).

For he will rescue you from every trap and protect you from deadly disease.—Psalm 91:3 (NLT).

Wow. We slept comforted, reassured, and downright amazed by the timing of their phone call and messages relayed to us on the very night of the diagnosis.

MORE LOVE ARRIVED AS time went on: from an offer to organize a meal rotation to arrival of hand-knitted textiles; to texts and calls, to lifted prayers, and visits.

Get-well cards descended inside the mailbox, the number quickly surpassing the space I allotted on two deep window ledges, each card accompanied by good wishes from pep talks, to favorite scriptures, to reminders of inner strength and courage, to enclosed gift cards, and promises of things to look forward to when better days arrive.

Hopes were shared for getting together soon. Two kinds of soup arrived at our door one evening, carried by Teresa who stood there holding them. Other days meant more delicious dishes, including nourishing and healthy homemade turkey soup from Brian's school colleague, Steve and wife, Cindy. Still more comfort came from Donna with her homemade chicken-noodle soup.

We were thought of—thoughts.

We were prayed for—prayers.

And they have meant the world to us. These tangible deeds and petitions to heaven are humbling. I think of the times I have fallen short, shorter-than short, in sending a card of cheer, stopping to pray for someone who comes to mind, slipping a fast-food gift card into the mail, ordering a plant, dropping a text message, and sometimes hardest of all in the face of crisis, calling a number.

What I've realized is that I can do better because it matters. What matters less is that while I have spent a career working with words, I am lousy, perplexed even, at *what* to write on get-well, or sympathy, or thinking-of-you cards.

I could write a lengthy essay on the topic of your choice faster than pen a few words of encouragement when someone is going through something awful. Everything I say feels trite. But to the recipients, what matters is the *doing of it*. Words of hope are *never* trite when they come from the heart and you read them during a low moment.

The point is to establish that we care and offer ... something ... a word, a deed, a prayer. What I've come to appreciate through all of this is how some folks simply don't take no for an answer.

Many ask, "What do you need?" I've asked that in these situations, too! People will usually say, "Not a thing, but thanks."

But those homemade scones that arrived in the mail from Brian's cousin Cate? A hand-assembled cancer notebook and binder made by Patty? The U.S. Postal Service delivering a recommended cancer cookbook from hometown classmate Krista, or from a number of teacher friends of Brian's sharing their personal favorite books?

It's all humbling and kind and priceless. I'm making a note to be like these people effective immediately. I will fail, but maybe I will sometimes succeed.

I AM AMAZED TO read the eloquent prose Brian has received inside the cards. For example:

Inserted inside Debbie's handmade card: "Some reminders from God's Word as you face this next phase in your cancer journey. God is unshakeable and that one fact is sufficient for us when we are feeling shakeable."

Valerie wished us peace, "in order for you to heal and regain your strength."

Handwritten inside Angela's card: "You would always tell me how strong I was. I did not feel it at the time, but it gave me courage to move forward. I am now telling you how strong you are, and a bit sassy (okay, a lot) as well. Allow others to care for you. There is always light after the dark."

Every week during months of this journey, a card arrived for Brian from my childhood church, each with a handwritten thought or two from Marie; other dear friends such as John and Debby and Sue sent weekly cards. Our own home church has been amazing with Pastor Keith setting his clock for six each evening to pray for us. He came to our home two days before Brian's surgery for prayer and anointing. That's not to mention my life group, Ovid Midlife Moms, or my community of Bible Study Fellowship prayer warriors.

And how we treasure those regular phone calls Brian has gotten from his brother, Steve, and dear friends John, Michael, Rick, Tom and others.

Then there are the candles, books, and puzzles. Word came that a gift basket would be arriving from a staff member from the school where Brian retired several years ago. There were actually two baskets and both bulged with love. The love was symbolized by words and wax.

The candles from friends Lyn and Julie were labeled with scriptures to brighten the darkest of our winter days and nights. The idea for this gift came after Brian had asked at the beginning of all this, during a dark autumn, if we had plenty of candles stowed away for the long winter ahead. I said we did. He responded, "Good, because I'm going to need them."

The cards will stay out for a while, stacked high and pressed down to make room for more in a big, wooden bowl at the center of our dining room table. The bowl is from my mother's house, and Grandma Jobe's home before her. Eventually the greeting cards will go into deeper storage. Yes, we'll keep them, same as we kept those from our other terrifying ordeal.

THIS ISN'T THE FIRST time we've learned about the value of thoughts and prayers. During the cleaning-out months, I came across a stack of cards from more than thirty years ago when our Sam, at eleven months, survived open-heart surgery.

During *that* dark winter, Sam received a diagnosis of a heart defect. The cardiologist explained the findings, not to us exactly, but more to medical students who filled the small hospital-examination room. We listened as he told them the news, their faces studying ours for reactions. It's an experience on my short list of worst life moments.

Tough information, stabs to your own heart when it's put to you that your baby requires open-heart surgery, or more recently, that your husband has cancer and needs the works to address it.

In Sam's case, in the midst of our devastation, Brian had the presence of mind to ask the one question with an answer we would cling to then.

"Can you fix him?"

"Yes."

Hope.

Our baby had a rough time, and after his surgery, things weren't looking good. Our pastor, along with several friends and family members, clasped hands and prayed with us, very specifically, for a miracle.

God knew our thoughts and answered our prayers.

Cards and letters gave us a boost. And that's why those were kept for more than three decades and will be kept longer still. I'm happy that Sam, who is thirty-five when I publish this, looked through each and every one, seeing the support that, while a baby, he and we had experienced.

IT IS GOOD FOR Brian to read the cards that arrive for him and know that on this side of heaven, in the midst of a time that feels the opposite of paradise, there are people who care, love us, and who want us to know that we are in their, yes—thoughts and prayers.

Are thoughts and prayers somehow an outdated offering as some suggest or mock in recent years? How so, I wonder. I'm grateful to those who don't see them as irrelevant.

We'll take all we can get of both, and if you don't want your share, send them our way!

For the Bible tells us that we're in God's thoughts:

For I know the plans I have for you," says the LORD. "They are plans for good and not for disaster, to give you a future and a hope. – Jeremiah 29:11 (NLT)

For the Bible tells us that we're in God's prayers:

And the Holy Spirit helps us in our weakness. For example, we don't know what God wants us to pray for. But the Holy Spirit prays for us with groanings that cannot be expressed in words. And the Father who knows all hearts knows what the Spirit is saying, for the Spirit pleads for us believers in harmony with God's own will. – Romans 8:26-27 (NLT)

Are thoughts and prayers somehow contrary to science? Of course not! We thank God for science! He invented it.

In the midst of suffering: the hope of heaven; the love of people—expressed through thoughts and prayers. And maybe also through a side dish of cousin Beth's homemade potato soup. It would pair nicely with cousin Cate's scones.

31

Now that it's done

BEFORE I SPENT MONTHS working on this book, I spent
months cleaning out. During that time, I attacked our home's
storage spaces and reminisced over stories and memories behind
the new-found objects. I decided what to do with many things we've
kept for years, and thought about the people associated with each
object.

You might be thinking about how amazing our house looks
now; how organized, pared down, and utterly free from clutter.
Lovely thoughts, but no. Editors from the home-design media are
not beating down our door for interviews or TV shows.

Ours is an ordinary household with the usual amount of ongoing
upkeep. We're retired. We're empty-nesters. We still get behind.

But there is a peace in knowing exactly what we have (two large
and two mini staplers, for example), being able to quickly put our
hands on supplies (extension cords are in the kitchen junk drawer
in the bottom cabinet left of the stove), and objects we don't want

have been released into a variety of directions (given away, recycled, or trashed).

THE MINUTE YOU ARE somewhat organized, it all starts unraveling. This is home life. Often there is a new mess to clean up, dirty dishes, clothes to wash, things that get put away in the wrong places or not at all. Sometimes I put heirlooms aside in special locations so that they won't be lost—but I do such a good job—I can't find them.

It's likely that if I return to the attic in a year, or shoot, even this minute, I'll find more things I'm willing to let go. That will continue because the longer we live, we're increasingly okay with the letting go of stuff. There were objects I got rid of during the process described in this book that I never dreamt I'd give up. But when the time is right, it's easier than I thought. It's good, even.

There's a popular mantra that people proclaim nowadays. It goes something like this: "I couldn't bear thinking of my kids inheriting all this stuff and having to deal with it. I should go ahead and get rid of it now."

My reaction to that is: only if you want to. Keep using and enjoying your belongings. Just don't expect that your descendants will feel about them as you do. I can tell you this: I don't care if my kids want any of our stuff. Much of it holds memories that aren't theirs. They have their own.

STILL, GETTING EVERYTHING ORGANIZED, eliminating excess or damaged items before someone else has to do that, is helpful. If the kids don't like what we saved, there are secondhand dealers, antiques-store owners, auction houses, donation sites, and garage sales. If they wish, someone will come and take it all away.

If you find yourself encouraged to go through your own storied stuff, and donate, keep, organize, or do as you otherwise see fit, may you find comfort that these touchstones provide in remembering and telling your life stories and expressing gratitude for God's varied means of provision.

I hope that you enjoy your homes, families, friends, communities, delight in your faith, and that you laugh a lot. *A whole lot.*

Inside the folder of no, I found the long-forgotten poem that follows. I wrote it in 1981.

Humble Junk

My house is done in Early Garage Sale.
I am not sorry; changing its look would make me wail.

It contains Grandma's lovely antiques,
Gifts from cherished friends, and on-sale uniques.

A sofa and chair with raggedy ends,
A coffee table whose middle bends.

But my house is welcome to those who pass by.
They are invited in—no need for a why.

Period furnishings they will not find.
Still my lived-in home will treat them kind.

An interior decorator I do not need.
I love my furnishings—it's true, indeed.

I would not trade my humble junk.
I might start a new trend—
With some kind of luck.

AND NOW, WITH THE attic, drawers, boxes, and bins in better order than they've ever been on my watch, it's time to move forward, grateful for the experiences, for the lessons learned, and for the memories revisited.

I wish you your *own* journey, complete with too many blessings to count. I guess it's time to head back down that ladder. You'll find it sturdier than when this process started! We ended up replacing it with a new aluminum one. It's ready for whatever trips back up the stairs we need to make.

I press on to reach the end of the race and receive the heavenly prize for which God, through Christ Jesus, is calling us.
–Philippians 3:14 (NLT)

EPILOGUE

--◦--⟨≡≡⟩--◦--

Making new memories

NOT LONG AFTER I completed writing the final chapter of this book, I returned to my hometown to serve as a bus hostess for a bicentennial-themed public tour of the county. I had been asked a couple months prior, and looked forward to it with great anticipation.

Drive me around the old stomping ground of my youth and I'm blissful, even though I hadn't lived there in forty-three years.

Kindred spirit Nancy Huntington had invited me to host. We didn't know each other as kids, but as adults, came to see that we feel the same about our home county, and we know many of the same people. We also share a bond that I never would have thought possible to even *be a bond* until we found it: both of us had been student office aides for the school principal, Mr. Cummins.

Nancy worked in the office during high school; years later the assignment somehow showed up on my class roster for eighth grade. I had never applied, nor been asked, if I wanted the position. It has always been a mystery how I landed it.

In seventh grade, I had gotten into trouble for talking in class. I know it's hard to believe, but I like to talk. Okay, so it's not hard to believe. The incident happened when Mr. Cummins substituted for our wonderful English teacher, Mrs. Myers. The entire class fell silent as we worked individually on our lessons with the principal watching from the teacher's desk.

Lost in thought, I couldn't recall the definition of the word "synonym." In a moment of totally forgetting the situation and *whose* eagle eye was upon us, I turned around to ask my neighbor to define the word.

"You," said the deep, authoritative voice of Mr. Cummins. "*You!*" he repeated. "To the office!"

I turned slowly around, realizing that by "*You*," he meant me.

In utter humiliation, I slinked to the office and sat in terror in the waiting area. Mrs. Miller, the school secretary (yes, that was her title), looked me over solemnly, no doubt wondering what Liberty Junior High School felony I had committed.

When Mr. Cummins came in, I followed him through the door into his inner office (or possibly through the gates of you know what), where I took a seat in front of his desk. I got quite the scolding. I reacted by sobbing! I was only a little sorry for talking, but much more, sorry that I had gotten in trouble. I sure didn't want him calling my parents. Mr. Cummins let me off with a lecture and I had the rest of the day to stew about if he phoned the folks.

He never called them. What is a good synonym for the word "relief?"

To have gotten sent to the principal in the seventh grade, then find myself chosen as an office aide the following school year seemed nothing short of a miracle.

HALF A CENTURY AGO, our county celebrated its one hundred fiftieth anniversary. The girls wore long, calico skirts or dresses made by their mothers or grandmothers. Some also sported matching bonnets. We couldn't wait to channel our inner pioneers and wear them to the festivities that unfolded in a carnival-like atmosphere all around the courthouse square.

Past met present as we hopped on the spider-type ride that lifted us into the air as our seats twirled and we viewed the town square in a new way.

The women wore sesquicentennial-belle pins with tiny, dangling, gold-toned bells. Following the celebration, Mom dropped the pin into her pink jewelry box and there it stayed, untouched for decades until it moved into mine.

I got it out and proudly wore it on the bicentennial bus tour. I wasn't alone, as another lady on our bus—the mother of a classmate—sported hers. It had been in her jewelry chest for half a century too.

The day of the tour, I noted that once again, the east side of the courthouse contained carnival-type booths. During the lunch break, we sat at tables steps away from the spot where half-a-century earlier, I had soared through the air in my prairie skirt.

So much has happened in the fifty years since. I finished growing up, got married, lived a few different places, had two sons, and a career. But what hasn't changed is an affection for those home places, for the folks there, and for that sublime feeling of stepping into a place where the belonging runs deep.

I'M REMINDED THAT HISTORY is a living thing, transforming itself from an event to a memory every day as the person makes a way through life. The bus tour added more memories.

We proudly learned more about our county's significant role in the Underground Railroad where enslaved people were helped to find freedom in Canada. We visited beautiful farms and toured landmarks. We saw not only the history of those places, but how they serve residents today.

The Liberty-belle pin is back inside my jewelry box. I didn't need to pick up a T-shirt or new pin this time around. The old pin is keepsake enough for both celebrations. Guess who hosted one of the other tour buses? None other than the *son* of Mr. Cummins. This is what you call a full-circle life experience.

It's the kind of thing that can happen when you clean out your attic, or read an old letter from a friend, or return to your hometown. I don't know exactly what else you call it. But I know that for me, a synonym would be "joy."

ALSO, IN THE WEEKS following completion of this manuscript, some updates emerge. Janet Leonard, a member of my writing group, told us that as writers, we're artists painting pictures with our pens. I bought us all pen-sized paint brushes to keep with our special writing utensils as reminders of her words. Mine is now in that ceramic holder I mention in the Pen pals chapter.

One of my favorite consignment shops has closed since I wrote the chapter where I mention my go-to clothing suppliers. By the time you read this book, it's hard to say how many more updates, both large and small, may have taken place.

Life keeps changing and our stories continue to unfold. Keep making memories. A book ends, but our lives are works in progress. Our possessions are temporary.

Enjoy your stuff within a proper perspective. But love God—and love people.

"Don't store up treasures here on earth, where moths eat them and rust destroys them, and where thieves break in and steal. Store your treasures in heaven, where moths and rust cannot destroy, and thieves do not break in and steal. Wherever your treasure is, there the desires of your heart will also be.

—Matthew 6:19-21 (NLT)

Readers' guide for book clubs

Book club gatherings are often enlightening and entertaining. Here are prompts for your own stories, experiences, and insights relating to chapters of this book.

ONE: Two of a kind

Questions: How do you and those in your household differ about the keeping of objects? If you could inherit anything from anyone in your family (traits, talents, or objects), what is it? How would you enjoy it?

Activities: Bring a keepsake and tell its story. Demonstrate to your group a talent that has to do with an heirloom. Examples: twirl your old baton; play a treasured tune on a childhood instrument such as a recorder. Show something you have made, such as a piece of pottery, jewelry, or handmade card.

TWO: Family artifacts aren't about price tags

Questions: What's the oddest or most humorous thing you keep? Why do we hold onto items that others might likely get rid of?

Activities: Show something that fits the above questions and explain its importance to you. Describe a historic site or home of a famous person that you visited. Pass around a brochure or a few photos from such a place. Plan group outing to your local or state historical society or to a house museum. Share coffee or a meal afterward and discuss.

THREE: The golden letter

Questions: Is there a non-family figure in your life who influenced or encouraged you in a special way? How so? Have you ever had a surprise invitation for an adventure, vacation, or job? Explain.

Activities: Show a postcard, invitation, or letter you've never forgotten. Go through old cards and letters. Reach out to someone who sent you one of those whom you haven't been in touch with for a long time. Describe what happened.

FOUR: On tap

Questions: Were you, or did you ever want to be, in a special group, club, or on a team such as dance, cheer, or other sports but you never got the opportunity? What childhood or past organizations did you join? Discuss if or how they shaped you.

Activities: Show a costume, uniform, or awards from your past and tell your experiences relating to them. Demonstrate a dance, song, cheer, or repeat a creed from one of those organizations or teams. As a child, did you ever save your money for something special? What?

FIVE: You do you

Questions: What's your favorite school-days-era life lesson? Did you ever "fail" at something, but learned a bigger lesson in the process?

Activities: Pass around a school-days photo of yourself and tell what you were like at that age. Think of a movie, TV show, or book that influenced you to be who you are today. Vote as a group on either one movie, TV show, or book mentioned in this discussion. Watch or read it at a meeting or on your own and discuss at a meeting.

SIX: Playing dress up

Questions: Was going to prom a big deal to you? Did you ever look forward to a big life event and then feel let down afterward? Explain.

Activities: Bring a picture of you in your prom or special-occasion outfit. Place it face down on a table upon your meeting arrival. Hostess will mix the photos and turn them over. Everyone will see if they can guess who goes with what photo.

SEVEN: Clothes call

Questions: Tell the group about your all-time favorite outfit. Why did you like it so much? What or where are your favorite resources for clothes shopping? (Specific stores, catalogs, online shopping, consignment, garage sale, etc.)

Activities: Bring the names and addresses of your favorite consignment or other stores or clothing catalogs to share. Plan a shopping trip with your club to some of the favorite retailers mentioned at your discussion. Have a clothing swap from items in your closet!

EIGHT: Here's hoping

Questions: Do you or someone in your family have a hope chest? If so, what do you keep inside? How do you display it? What compromises have you made with a spouse or loved one about keeping belongings? What is one question you would like to ask your parents, grandparents or other ancestors?

Activities: Bring something from inside your cedar chest or other storage space and share about it. Take a photo and discuss a useful or unique way you store keepsake items.

NINE: Their best advice

Questions: What is the best advice you ever received? What is the best advice you ever gave? When has life "thrown you" and how did you "get back on the horse?"

Activities: Bring a photo of yourself showcasing a special moment, surprise skill, or activity. (Maybe you were a rodeo champion; received a scholarship for academics or athletics; were prom queen; won a trophy for something your friends today don't know about.) Plan a field trip or evening out where a new skill is explored: a paint or ceramics class; attending a library program on home decorating; a yoga or exercise class, or a cooking demonstration.

TEN: A folder full of no

Questions: Have you ever applied for an opportunity you thought you had no chance at getting, but you landed it? Explain. Would you rather take a chance on a difficult, challenging job that seems over your head or a lesser job you feel confident doing? Were you ever inspired to accomplish something because of negative feedback? Explain and tell how that worked.

Activities: Bring or explain a rejection or acceptance letter you received, or a letter of any kind recognizing or praising you in some way that meant a lot. Tell about an unexpected "yes" from your life when you were perhaps expecting a "no."

ELEVEN: Thinking inside the box

Questions: Do you ever hold onto old technology because it still works or you think you'll need it someday? What one thing do you have a tendency to collect too much of? Boxes? Earrings? Craft supplies? Plants?

Activities: Talk about or bring to show an old piece of technology that you still own and can't part with. Round up all your miscellaneous cords and tech plugs, etc. Return them to your tech provider or recycle. Take a photo of what you had and share. Or, see if someone in your group would agree in advance to appropriately dispose of these if members bring them. Pile them up to see what you have and discuss why you are now releasing them.

TWELVE: Speaking of boxes

Questions: Did anyone ever insult your abilities or competence? Have you ever been taken aback by a special compliment?

Activities: Share about your first paid job. If someone asked you to give a talk or program about something, such as a talent or area of expertise, what would it be?

THIRTEEN: Let sleeping bags lie

Questions: Do you keep something in your home that everyone pokes fun at (or would, if they knew you had it) yet remains surprisingly useful? What?

Activities: Bring in an example from the question above. Have a swap meet! Bring something you keep that would make a fun white-elephant gift. Wrap it up, swap it, and wait for the laughs!

FOURTEEN: To keep or not to keep?

Questions: Have you ever recycled or transformed an heirloom into a different keepsake (with fabric, etc.)? What's a keepsake others think you should keep that you got rid of?

Activities: Bring in something to share that you transformed or upcycled into something different. Tell about specific plans you have to recycle or upcycle an object you keep.

FIFTEEN: Pen pals

Questions: Do you have a stash of writing utensils? What's most unusual?

Activities: Bring a sentimental pen or pencil that you save and explain it. Clean out your junk drawers and bring in all the writing utensils you no longer want. Exchange them with each other or drop off at a nonprofit that could use them.

SIXTEEN: Jamming with the shredder

Questions: Do you keep something because someone told you that you should? What? How do you decide to retain or destroy your important papers? If you shred your papers, do you do anything with the shreds such as use them in packing, etc.?

Activities: Have a shredding night! Ask for volunteers to bring their portable shredders. Members can bring an item or file to shred that they have been hesitant to part with, or maybe something they would love to finally bid farewell to by shredding. Then they will ceremoniously shred their papers! Tell about how you store old paperwork or if you retain a paper trail. How do you manage important papers?

SEVENTEEN: Screen cleaning

Questions: How do you care for the screens in your life? Do you have a cybersecurity provider that you especially like? Have you ever been hacked? Do you keep a written passcode list for all your applicable technology?

Activities: Bring in a photograph or the actual technology or gadget you keep that you never had to worry about in days gone by regarding cybersecurity. Is there anything you keep in old-school fashion because you don't trust internet or other storage?

EIGHTEEN: The last address book?

Questions: Do you regularly use an address book? Do you think address books are relics of the past?

Activities: Send a note, via snail-mail, to someone in your life whose address is inside your book. Tell who you chose and why. Tell about their response.

NINETEEN: What's in your bag?

Questions: If you could keep only one bag of belongings, what would you want in it? What things can never be available on a phone that you always want to keep in tangible form?

Activities: Bring something that would go into your bag. Everyone can arrive at the meeting with their one thing hidden inside a sack. For roll call, go around and each person reveal what's inside.

TWENTY: Postcards and property; dishes and diamonds

Questions: Have you ever met anyone famous? Who and how? Does someone in your life story have an interesting experience that others would enjoy hearing about regarding a brush with someone famous or with history?

Activities: If you have a photo of yourself with a famous person, bring it and show. Bring a postcard you sent, received, or is of historic importance to your family. Explain.

TWENTY-ONE: Getting carried away

Questions: If you are attached to something due to its past, can you let it go in the present? Do you travel lightly? How or how not?

Activities: Bring a vacation photo of somewhere you went long ago. Tell what you carried inside your luggage on that trip. Did you travel lightly or over pack? Did you pack anything back then that we no longer use today such as garter belts or curlers?

TWENTY-TWO: One woman's trash

Questions: Have you ever given something away to a person who seemed thrilled to get it? What was that like? How do you feel about hosting garage sales?

Activities: Explain any garage-sale finds or experiences that stand out. Bring a photo of something wonderful you bought secondhand.

TWENTY-THREE: Showers of memories

Questions: Were you given any bridal showers? Thoughts about those? Are you familiar with the tradition of a bow bouquet? Explain.

Activity: Bring something you got at your bridal shower that you still use.

TWENTY-FOUR: Shelf life

Questions: If you have a family Bible, is family history recorded there? Do you keep books because they belonged to family members?

Activities: Show and tell about a book that you keep for historical or sentimental reasons. Look inside an old family Bible. What interesting or unexpected information is recorded or tucked inside?

TWENTY-FIVE: Leaving us in stitches

Questions: What traditions are in your family regarding handmade textiles?

Activity: Bring in some type of homemade textile, such as a tablecloth, apron, quilt, Christmas stocking, or afghan that you value.

TWENTY-SIX: Not much of a spice girl

Questions: Take the challenge at the end of this chapter. How old are your herbs and spices? Any outdated? What's your most-used herb or spice?

Activity: Do a fun competition at your meeting. Everyone can bring her oldest, outdated herb or spice. Give a prize for the most outdated.

TWENTY-SEVEN: Christmas trees tell stories of our lives

Questions: If you have a Christmas tree, how do you decorate it? Do you have a tradition regarding decorating your home for the holidays?

Activities: Bring a favorite ornament and tell why it's special to you. Or, bring a photo of a memorable Christmas tree from any time in your life and tell about it.

TWENTY-EIGHT: The prodigy

Questions: Did you have a special skill or show a unique talent for something as a young child, or in your earlier years? Tell members about it. Did you continue enjoying it long-term in life? What special talent have you always wished you had?

Activity: Bring something artsy you made or an instrument that you play.

TWENTY-NINE: Mothers are keepers

Questions: What special things have you kept that were your children's? What belongings of yours did you discover that your parents kept?

Activity: Bring something to show that belongs to one of your children or to you as a child that you aren't likely to let go.

THIRTY: Thoughts and prayers

Questions: Have you ever been touched by the thoughts and prayers of others? How so? In what particular ways have people offered you comfort in your time of trouble? Any favorite story, gift, or scripture to share?

Activities: Explain something you might offer someone when they could use cheering or a hand, such as a particular meal and method in which you provide it (delivered by you; gift card), a special service, etc.

THIRTY-ONE: Now that it's done

Questions: How has this book changed your outlook on cleaning out or paring down your own belongings? Do you plan to do that, and if so, how, when, and why? Is there a takeaway you'd like to share about this book or about your own situation or philosophy about the "stuff" of life?

Activity: Choose any prompt from the above chapters mentioned and share it at your meeting.

Author's note: Share your thoughts on the book, or about your book club discussions. Let's connect via email at: newsgirl.1958@gmail.com; on Facebook at the Donna Cronk author page, or website: donnacronk.com.

ACKNOWLEDGMENTS

Writing and publishing this book took a year. Assembling material for it required a lifetime. There are a good many people who contributed in a variety of ways whether they know it or not. I'm grateful to everyone who permitted use of their names in stories and for the resulting essays and memories associated with them.

God knew that during a season of personally challenging months, I needed a project. Cleaning out the attic was just the beginning. Not only did we get a clean attic, but I found ideas for a follow-up project—which became the book you are holding. I credit the good Lord for prompting me to see this as a new, exciting adventure.

Even though I did the writing, it's Brian Cronk who serves not only as my husband, but my inspiration. He whole-heartedly supports my need to put words together and is my biggest cheerleader. I'm immeasurably blessed by his love and laughter.

I'm grateful to the New Castle *Courier-Times*, my employer of thirty-one years, and to Paxton Media LLC, for the privilege of telling true stories, including my own in personal columns, on the pages of the newspaper, and in related publications during all those years. I appreciate their permission to retell some or parts of my previous slice-of-life columns within this memoir.

Special thanks to current *Courier-Times* editor, Travis Weik, for his support and kindness.

Thank you Marilyn Witt, for not hesitating to say yes when asked to create a beautiful cover—the face of this project. You are as gracious as you are talented, and a treasure to many, including to me.

Thank you photographer David Burns for your technical expertise.

I'm blessed by two designated editors who read, reacted to, and cared for my manuscript with corrections and suggestions. Thank you Debbie McCray for looking at this memoir The McCray Way, through the lens of your engineering mind and tender heart. Your suggested edits and thought-provoking questions strengthen the work.

Thank you Becky Radford, whose eagle eye found things I overlooked, such as the difference between verses and versus. I would be remiss not to thank her husband, my longtime colleague and friend, Darrel Radford, for his good sense in marrying her or I would never know this "smartest girl in the school."

I suspect that both these women were the smartest girls in their respective schools. But they keep it humble and would never tell you that.

Another thank you goes to Lisa Perry for batting cleanup with editing insights.

Big shout out to Writer Chicks Janet Leonard, Cathy Shouse, and Susan Sparks for our brain trust regarding all-things writing and publishing.

When counting blessings, I also think of the following writers, authors, and friends who inspire and cheer me on during this process. Thank you in alphabetical order to Cheryl K. Bennett, Christina Ryan Claypool, Katie Clontz, Steve Dicken, Blaise Doubman, Sandy Moore, Janis Thornton, and Tina West.

Thank you to the roster of the Ovid Midlife Moms (okay, we're still midlife in *spirit*). Sending love to each on the roster as of this printing for their life support and sisterhood: co-founder Delaine Wooden, Sharon Adams, Karen Baker, Karen Carr, Naomi Davis, Teresa Dowers, Terri Fredericks, Linda Mackey, Donna Shields, Marilyn Sullivan, Rita Teeters, and Sandi Voss. Also, to charter member Patty Redmond of our Colorado bureau.

Thank you to longtime friends Dr. Sue Anderson, Patti Broshar-Foust, Suzy Castrodale, Gay Kirkton, Char Kuhn, Julie Mc Duffee, and Debby Williams. Thank you all for your continued friendships and support.

Thank you to my brother-in-law Steve Cronk for the funniest thing you ever said to me, which I put in the book. My love always to sons Sam and Ben. Appreciation goes to my sisters-in-law, Linda Cronk and Jeannie Jobe for use of stories that include them.

Shout out to a few more from my original hometown: nieces Lisa Norris and Marlene Thompson; friends Shirley and Beth McCoy, Lois Frasur, Melody Gault, Nancy Huntington, and John Estridge. Also, to Cheryl Mills, best friend of my youth, and teacher Jeanne Sipahigil.

There are others, and it will be painful to find that I omitted their names once this is in print. A special thank you to the unexpected people who come beside me with opportunities, support, and invitations into their worlds and their book clubs, if only for an evening, and sometimes, for much longer.

I'm also thinking of those who have passed on, but whose influence remains a part of my heart.

Appreciation extends to readers of *The Courier-Times* and *Her Magazine for Women*, and to those who read my novels for their continued support and encouragement. Thank you for every opportunity and every kind word.

Thank You, Father God, for Your goodness, mercy, and for the Provision of Your Son, Jesus Christ.

ABOUT THE AUTHOR

Lifelong Indiana resident Donna Cronk has been interested in writing since childhood. Reared on the family's Union County farm, Cronk earned a journalism degree from Indiana State University.

She is a career community-newspaper journalist, first at the Attica paper, currently named *The Fountain County Neighbor*, then thirty-one years at the New Castle *Courier-Times* where she also edited *Her Magazine for Women*. She has been recognized with numerous statewide writing awards.

Cronk spent much of 2021 penning the memoir, *There's a Clydesdale in the Attic: Reflections on Keeping and Letting Go*. She is author of two inspirational novels, *Sweetland of Liberty Bed & Breakfast* and *That Sweet Place: At Home in the Heartland*.

Married to Brian, who spent his career in secondary education, the couple have two adult sons: Sam and Ben.

A Pendleton, Indiana resident, Cronk is active in her church where she is part of a women's life group and is also in a service ministry. She co-founded a small writing group, Writer Chicks, and has been a Bible Study Fellowship student for many years. The author enjoys providing uplifting, slightly humorous programs for women's gatherings and book discussion groups.

When she's not writing her Next Chapter newspaper column, Cronk enjoys time with her husband and loved ones, and connecting with readers at book-related venues. She especially enjoys travels to historic sites, and counts a trip to Israel among her favorite life experiences.

Connect with Cronk on Facebook at her Donna Cronk author page, on her website, donnacronk.com, and by email, donna@donnacronk.com.

ABOUT THE COVER ARTIST

Indiana artist Marilyn Witt lives on a farm in southern Henry County, Indiana surrounded by nature and the rural scenery that inspires her pastel and oil paintings.

Her style is impressionistic, rich in color and filled with light, mood, and spontaneity. She exhibits in national, regional, and local shows, winning top awards.

Witt's paintings are on the covers of four novels, and one children's book, along with this memoir, and has been featured in *Her Magazine for Women*. She has been awarded Signature Membership in International Plein Air Painters where she is a regional ambassador.

The artist is a member of a number of national and local art organizations. Her paintings are included in private and corporate collections in Indiana, Florida, Texas, Pennsylvania, New Mexico, Kentucky, Arizona, and India. Her work may be seen at the Brown County Art Gallery, 1 Artist Drive, Nashville, Indiana.

Witt is married to Dennis and they are parents of two. They enjoy their family, which also includes grandchildren and great-grandchildren. Witt is also active in her church and in her community.

For more information, visit marilynwittart.com. Email Witt at mjw4arts@nltc.net.

Made in the USA
Monee, IL
15 June 2022

98048772R00115